T0385365

CHARLES DICKENS

THIS IS AN ANDRE DEUTSCH BOOK

First published in 2011 by André Deutsch, this edition published 2019

An imprint of the Carlton Publishing Group

20 Mortimer Street

London

W1T 3JW

Text © Lucinda Hawksley 2011, 2019

Design © André Deutsch Limited 2019

ISBN 978 0 233 00605 5

Printed in Dubai

CHARLES DICKENS

THE MAN, THE NOVELS, THE VICTORIAN AGE

ANDRE
DEUTSCH

Two centuries after he was born, Charles Dickens remains as famous as he was in his lifetime. His name is recognizable all over the world and his books have never been out of print. Dickens is remembered today as one of the most famous men in history, but he was born into an ignominious lower-class family and struggled through an impoverished childhood and the shame of his family being imprisoned. Charles Dickens was a truly self-made man – but he never forgot the lessons his childhood had taught him and he strove to bring about change. Although best known as a novelist, he was also a tireless campaigning journalist and the editor of two popular magazines *Household Words* and *All The Year Round*.

Dickens wanted to help bring about sanitary reform, gender equality, more efficient hospitals, prison reform and education for all. Long before Freud was born, Dickens was making psychological analyses of his characters and how their past shaped their future. He also looked at the roles that poverty and despair played in crime – a connection most politicians were reluctant to make.

In writing this book I was fascinated by the many facets that made up Dickens's complicated and charismatic personality. In addition to his roles as father, husband, friend, lover, sibling and son, there were so many other interests that filled his already busy life, such as his love of acting, his longing to travel the world and his secret desire to be a detective.

It may be two hundred years since Dickens was born, but his work remains relevant not only because his plots and characters still have the ability to make us laugh and cry, but because the problems he fought against, and which he wrote about so poignantly, still exist. The essence of almost all Dickens' writing was the belief that those with money, power and influence need to take responsibility for those who are disenfranchised. Imagine how different our societies could be today if this belief was genuinely put into practice.

LUCINDA DICKENS HAWKSLEY

CONTENTS

1

EARLY YEARS

In June 1809, John Dickens, a clerk in the Navy Pay Office, set up home with his new wife, Elizabeth (née Barrow). Having married in London, where the Barrow family lived, the couple arrived in Portsmouth, Hampshire, soon after the wedding. Their first marital home was at 387 Mile End Terrace, on the outskirts of the city.

John and Elizabeth's first child, Frances ("Fanny") Elizabeth Dickens, was born in 1810. Two years later, on 7 February 1812, their eldest son, Charles John Huffam Dickens, was born. Although six more siblings would follow, Charles never grew as close to any of them as he was to Fanny.

The family moved regularly, first within Portsmouth and then, in 1815, to London when John's job demanded it. Two years later John was relocated to the Navy Pay Office at Chatham Dockyard, in Kent, and the family moved once more. Charles Dickens's overwhelming childhood memories were of being in Kent, a county he loved; when he wrote in his novels about the countryside, it was often Kent that was in his mind as he created his landscapes on paper.

Charles's first teacher was his mother, an intelligent woman who taught him not only the basics of reading and writing but also, as his education progressed, Latin. At the age of six, he went with Fanny to a "dame school", a common practice of the time.

In 1821, the young Charles was sent to a school he would remember with fondness, run by an enthusiastic and well-educated man in his twenties named William Giles. It was at around this time, aged nine, that Dickens wrote his first work of fiction, a tragic play entitled *Miznar, the Sultan of India* (sadly, this juvenilia no longer exists). He was to spend just a few terms at William Giles's school, during which time his family's fortunes were steadily declining. John Dickens was in debt: he had borrowed a large amount from an acquaintance and found himself incapable of making the repayments.

John and Elizabeth Dickens were both outgoing, fun-loving people who enjoyed all the pleasures of the Regency era during which they had grown up. Elizabeth, continuing the musical entertainments of her childhood, would often relate how she went to a dance in Portsmouth while heavily pregnant with Charles and

OPPOSITE Charles Dickens was born in this house in Southsea, Portsmouth, in 1812. It is now a museum, furnished as it would have been when John and Elizabeth Dickens set up their home here.

went into labour there from the exertion. The couple found it impossible to live on the constraints of John's salary and never truly understood their finances.

Both parents would appear as characters in their son's novels: John was famously immortalized as Mr Micawber in *David Copperfield* and Elizabeth helped to inspire a number of characters, including aspects of Mrs Nickleby in *Nicholas Nickleby*. There were times when the novelist could be particularly harsh about his mother, but it would be wrong to say he saw only her flaws. There are many occasions, in letters as well as in creating his characters, when his admiration for her upbeat, flamboyant personality – as well as her strength in dealing with adversity – comes to the fore.

The family's monetary worries were exacerbated by a forced move to London in 1822, when John Dickens's office was transferred to Somerset House. This meant that he and his family needed to live in London, the most expensive part of England, but with a salary that did not make any allowances for the new location. Falling further

Dame Schools

These small village schools were run by women – often in their later years – who had no formal training in education, but who could read and write and who charged a very small fee. They usually took children up to the age of 14. Dickens would later parody this type of schooling in his writing.

into debt was inevitable. They moved to Bayham Street, in Camden Town (north London), where Elizabeth tried to raise extra money by opening a school. No pupils arrived and the Dickenses' finances continued to sink even lower. At first, Charles was left in Chatham with William Giles for a short while, but when the money for his school fees ran out, he went to London to live with his family. He was miserable about leaving his school and friends.

OPPOSITE TOP Charles's mother Elizabeth Dickens (1789–1863) was born Elizabeth Barrow. She and John Dickens (1785–1851) named their eldest son after her father, Charles Barrow (1759–1826).

ABOVE The Dickens family lived at 16 Bayham Street in Camden Town (the house is now demolished). Dickens would later name a character in *Bleak House* Mr Bayham Badger.

LEFT Charles's father John Dickens, second son of William Dickens (1719–85), a steward at Crewe Hall in Cheshire, and Elizabeth (née Ball, 1745–1824). William died when John was still a baby.

2

DEBT & SHAME

*By the start of 1824, John Dickens's financial situation was desperate and
it soon became obvious that Charles would need to start earning money.
Days after his 12th birthday, an opportunity for work arose.*

Throughout the early years of Charles's childhood, his mother's widowed sister, Mary Allen, had lived with the family. In 1821, she had married the widowed Dr Matthew Lamert, a surgeon with three sons. His eldest boy, James Lamert, had befriended Charles – but ironically, it was he who came up with the suggestion that would blight the little boy's childhood. James had recently become a clerk for Warren's Blacking Factory and found his young step-cousin a position there. The misery of this time would be confided to Charles's friend John Forster (1812–76) many years later, and revealed in Forster's *Life of Charles Dickens* (c.1872–74):

It is wonderful to me how I could have been so easily cast away at such an age. It is wonderful to me, that, even after my descent into the poor little drudge I had been since we came to London, no one had compassion enough on me – a child of singular abilities, quick, eager, delicate, and soon hurt, bodily or mentally – to suggest that something might have been spared, as certainly it might have been, to place me at any common school. Our friends, I take it, were tired out. No one made any sign. My father and mother were quite satisfied. They could hardly have been more so, if I had been twenty years of age, distinguished at a grammar-school, and going to Cambridge.

Shortly after Charles began working at Warren's, John Dickens was arrested for debt. He and his family – apart from Charles and his elder sister, Fanny, who was a boarding pupil at the Royal Academy of Music – were imprisoned at the Marshalsea Debtors' Prison in Southwark, south London. At this time it was the practice to incarcerate debtors along with their family and dependents. It was a nonsensical system whereby the debtor was unable to leave the prison to work, yet they needed to find the money to pay rent and upkeep to the prison for themselves and their family. The bonus, however, was that the prison kept the debtor safely out of the reach of angry creditors. In order to pay their costs, the debtor needed someone to support them financially. The onus of paying the family's costs fell on John and Elizabeth's eldest son, and much of Charles's meagre "six or seven" shillings a week went to support his family.

There were two Warren's premises: one at "30, Strand", which was owned by Robert Warren, and another at the nearby and confusingly named "30, Hungerford Stairs, Strand", which was run by his uncle Jonathan Warren. At the time Charles Dickens was working for Jonathan Warren, the uncle and nephew were embroiled in a furious legal battle. Charles worked ten hours a day, six days a week,

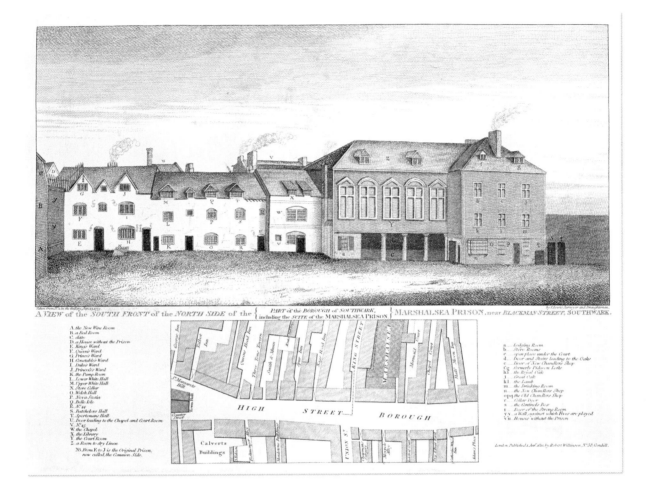

wrapping the blacking bottles and pasting labels onto them. He worked alongside two other boys: Paul "Poll" Green and Bob Fagin.

Initially, Charles was sent to lodge with a landlady in Camden Town, but the house, on Little College Street, was a long walk from his work and a very long walk from his family. Charles was so unhappy in his isolation that his parents arranged to have him moved to a lodging house in Lant Street, Southwark, a short distance from the prison. Lant Street would appear in *The Pickwick Papers* as the place where Bob Sawyer lived.

Dickens returned to this period of his childhood many times in his fiction, the most obvious reference being in *David Copperfield*. He was haunted by his experiences at Warren's – there are references to blacking bottles, often just a passing comment, in almost all his writings.

In *The Pickwick Papers*, Dickens made two scathing allusions to Warren's. Sam Weller works as a boot black at the White Hart Inn in Southwark, and Dickens tells the reader: "Mr Samuel brushed away with such hearty good-will ... [and] with a polish which would have struck envy to the soul of the amiable Mr Warren (for they used Day & Martin at the White Hart)." Knowing that Warren's warehouse employed copywriters called "poets", Dickens disparages Warren's again, during a conversation between Sam and his father. The older

Mr Weller warns his son: "Poetry's unnat'ral; no man ever talked poetry 'cept a beadle on boxin'-day, or Warren's blackin', or Rowland's oil, or some of them low fellows."

On 28 May 1824, John Dickens was released from the Marshalsea, but it would be some time before Charles was released from his imprisonment. A month later, his sister Fanny was awarded a silver medal from the Royal Academy of Music – meanwhile, Charles was still sitting at his table in the window of the blacking factory, aware of strangers gawping at him as he worked. He longed to leave work immediately but his mother had suggested he may as well continue working and keep his salary coming in for the family, as he would write later in an unfinished autobiography: "I do not write resentfully or angrily: for I know all these things have worked together to make me what I am: but I never afterwards forgot, I never shall forget, I never can forget, that my mother was warm for my being sent back."

The reprieve finally arrived some months later and Charles was whisked from the world of child labour back into the world of education. He was desperate to ensure that his new school friends should never come to hear about the shame of his time at Warren's.

Charles's new school was Wellington House Academy, run by an unpleasant schoolmaster named William Jones. Dickens later described him as "by far the most ignorant man I have ever had the pleasure to know ... one of the worst-tempered men perhaps that ever lived". The school was a world away from the happy times with William Giles in Chatham, but even a bullying headmaster was a welcome change from the drudgery of working at Warren's.

In 1827, the family experienced another financial crisis. They were evicted from their home, and Charles and Fanny were taken out of school, this time for good. In May of 1827, at the age of 15, Charles began working as a legal clerk in the firm of Ellis and Blackmore, in Gray's Inn, an area of London that appears many times in his novels. His first day was distinguished by being sent on an errand and coming back with a black eye, having got into a fight on the way. He worked for Ellis and Blackmore until the end of 1828, when he began a brief period of working for another legal firm, Charles Molloy.

I became, at ten years old, a little labouring hind in the service of Murdstone and Grinby. Murdstone and Grinby's warehouse was at the waterside. It was down in Blackfriars. Modern improvements have altered the place; but it was the last house at the bottom of a narrow street, curving down hill to the river, with some stairs at the end, where people took boat. It was a crazy old house with a wharf of its own, abutting on the water when the tide was in, and on the mud when the tide was out, and literally overrun with rats. Its panelled rooms, discoloured with the dirt and smoke of a hundred years, I dare say; its decaying floors and staircase; the squeaking and scuffling of the old grey rats down in the cellars; and the dirt and rottenness of the place; are things, not of many years ago, in my mind, but of the present instant. They are all before me, just as they were in the evil hour when I went among them for the first time, with my trembling hand in Mr Quinion's.

DAVID COPPERFIELD

OPPOSITE Warren's Blacking Factory was at the edge of the River Thames, at 30 Hungerford Stairs, the Strand. There was no bridge in Dickens's time, so a ferry took people across the river.

LEFT Wellington House Academy, attended by Dickens from 1824 until 1827, inspired Salem House in *David Copperfield*. Charles and his schoolmates kept white pet mice in their desks.

The Ubiquity of Blacking

As its name suggests, blacking was a black liquid, which could be used for many different purposes – to create one or other type of black finish – and was indispensable in a Victorian household or business. One form was used to polish black shoes, boots and other leather goods, such as saddles or carriage hoods. There was also another liquid known as "lead blacking" which was used to clean stoves, steps, fireplaces and cooking ranges. In the *London Directory* of 1823, Jonathan Warren is listed as the "Original Inventor of the Blacking sold under that Name". The most famous member of the family, however, was his nephew and rival Robert Warren, who is listed as "the inventor of Japan liquid blacking".

3

SKETCHES BY BOZ

If Charles Dickens had originally intended to work his way up and study for the law, his two years as a legal clerk altered his decision. He was frustrated by the legal world, which he described as "very dull".

His maternal uncle, John Henry Barrow, was a successful journalist and, since his release from prison, John Dickens had reinvented himself as a journalist, so Charles was encouraged to make use of his family's contacts. He trained as a stenographer and began working as a freelance court reporter in 1829. His experience of covering court cases for newspapers confirmed his beliefs about the legal world, a world he would criticize and parody with great intelligence in his fiction, most famously in *Bleak House*.

One of Dickens's earliest clients was a newspaper called the *Mirror of Parliament*. Reporting on the daily activities of Parliament helped to raise his awareness of social problems and injustices, and by 1832, he was also writing for a new and radical paper, the *True Sun*. It was at around this time that he began working on a series of short stories. The very first of his works of fiction to be published was "A Dinner at Poplar Walk" (which Dickens himself had entitled "A Sunday Out of Town"). It was published in the *Monthly Magazine*, and the author received no payment for it. For Dickens, however, the joy of being published was payment enough. As he recalled later, he had dropped the story through the office letterbox one evening "with fear and trembling". He had no way of knowing if the editor liked it until he bought an issue of the magazine and saw his story in print. Holding the magazine, Dickens "walked down to Westminster Hall, and turned into it for half an hour, because my eyes were so dimmed with joy and pride that they could not bear the street, and were not fit to be seen there". The editor commissioned a further eight stories – "sketches of everyday life".

By 1850, Dickens would be less pleased with his early work, writing contemptuously of these early stories as being "extremely crude and ill-considered, and bearing obvious marks of haste and inexperience"; like many writers, he came to be embarrassed by the work of his youth. Contemporary reviewers, however, agreed with the old *Monthly Magazine*'s editor and wrote glowing accounts of the work by this new and unknown writer: "The graphic descriptions … invest all he describes with amazing reality," wrote the reviewer for the *Morning Post*, continuing, "He has infinite skill in giving importance to the commonplace scenes of everyday occurrence." This skill, recognized so early on, would continue to define Dickens's work.

OPPOSITE This illustration for "The Great Winglebury Duel" appeared in the first series of *Sketches by Boz*. Dickens would later turn his short story into a farcical play, *The Strange Gentleman*.

George Cruikshank

Mrs Tibbs was, beyond all dispute, the most tidy, fidgety, thrifty little personage that ever inhaled the smoke of London; and the house of Mrs Tibbs was, decidedly the neatest in all Great Coram-street.... Mr Tibbs was by no means a large man. He had, moreover, very short legs, but, by way of indemnification, his face was peculiarly long. He was to his wife what the 0 is in 90 – he was of some importance WITH her – he was nothing without her.

SKETCHES BY BOZ

ABOVE On this title page of *Sketches by Boz*, the two figures depicted waving to the crowd below from the basket of a hot-air balloon are based on Dickens and illustrator Cruikshank.

While writing these stories for the *Monthly Magazine*, for which he received no fee, Dickens met – and impressed – a Mr John Payne Collier, subeditor of the *Morning Chronicle*. In a matter of months, Collier offered Dickens a job, and by August 1834, the young journalist had been taken on as a parliamentary reporter. His salary was five guineas a week. The *Morning Chronicle* secured Dickens's future. Within a month, he had a taste of adventure when he was sent on an epic journey from London to Edinburgh. It engendered within him a love of travelling that would endure until the end of his life. Dickens's work impressed his editors immediately and within a few weeks he was being asked to concentrate on a series of fictional "sketches" of everyday life in London; he wrote this non-journalistic work under the pseudonym of Boz. Less than two months after starting at the *Morning Chronicle*, Dickens was earning an extra two guineas a week writing similar "sketches" for the *Evening Chronicle*, under the new editorship of George Hogarth.

Boz's short stories were published in several magazines before publisher John Macrone came up with the idea of collecting them into a book. The result, *Sketches by Boz*, proved an undreamed-of success with the reading public. The first edition, illustrated by George Cruikshank, was published in February 1836, shortly before the first instalment of *The Pickwick Papers* appeared in print. Fourteen months later, the publishing house Chapman & Hall bought the copyright of *Sketches by Boz* from Macrone for the unprecedented sum of £2,000, and began reissuing the stories as monthly instalments.

In 1837, John Macrone died very suddenly, at the age of 28. To raise money for Macrone's widow and children, Dickens collaborated with a number of writers on an anthology entitled *The Pic-Nic Papers*, for which he wrote

Charles Dickens.

Geo Cruikshank

of ordinary people doing everyday things; the humour came not from grand farces, but from the minutiae of simple misunderstandings and comic situations. The stories were largely humorous, such as "The Bloomsbury Christening", but there were also serious, poignant tales including "The Drunkard's Death".

LEFT This sketch of the young Dickens by George Cruikshank shows the author as he looked at the start of his career – resembling a Regency dandy rather than a Victorian gentleman.

The Original Boz

Dickens took his pseudonym from his youngest brother's childhood nickname. Augustus Dickens became known in the family as Moses, which – according to Dickens's first biographer, John Forster – the family pronounced in a nasal way, as though they had a cold, making it sound like "Boses"; this became Boz.

Augustus was 15 years younger than Charles and grew up idolizing his older brother. As a teenager and young man he was a willing errand boy and accomplice, and Charles was desperate to get him away from what he saw as the bad influence of their father. When Augustus left school, Charles found him lodgings and a good job; he was desperately disappointed when Augustus gave up the job for a wild scheme reminiscent of one of John Dickens's ventures.

the introduction and contributed one of his works, "The Lamplighter's Story".

It is difficult for modern readers to understand the importance of *Sketches by Boz*, but for readers and critics in the 1830s, the stories broke new ground. Published at the end of the Georgian era, when Britain was poised on the brink of the Victorian age, the stories were a world away from the usual style of literature. Instead of gothic horror, romances in country houses and deep political polemics, Boz's stories focused on the middle and lower classes, looking at a London seldom visited in literature. This was not the London of aristocrats and grand houses, but a city

4

FIRST LOVE: MARIA BEADNELL

At the age of 17, Charles Dickens met the pretty eldest daughter of a wealthy banker. Maria Beadnell was two years older than her suitor and her parents did not approve of the match.

Dickens was an unknown with his way to make in the world and no wealthy family connections. The teenagers conducted a clandestine romance, with Dickens sending Maria passionate letters in secret, although his feelings of adoration were never truly reciprocated. Their accomplices were Maria's sister Anne and her fiancé Henry Kolle, with whom Dickens became very friendly.

By 1832, Maria's parents had become concerned enough about the unsuitable alliance to send her away to Paris. Some months later, after she had returned to London, Dickens ended the relationship. In his letter he wrote of a "painful struggle" to make her love him: "Our meetings of late have been little more than so many displays of heartless indifference on one hand while on the other they have never failed to prove a fertile source of wretchedness and misery ... I have engaged in a pursuit which has long since been worse than hopeless."

Dickens remained emotionally scarred by his unhappy love affair. In the late 1840s, Maria inspired the character of Dora in *David Copperfield*, the beautiful, carefree, selfish child bride. Dora is the ruling passion of David's early adulthood and they marry despite their obvious incompatibility – it is a cautionary tale from Dickens to male readers not to marry just because a woman is sexually alluring.

In 1855, when Charles and his wife Catherine were becoming painfully aware of how much they had grown apart, the author was thrilled to receive a letter from a Mrs Winter (Maria's married name). In his reply Dickens wrote: "Believe me, you cannot more tenderly remember our old days and our old friends than I do ... I forget nothing of these times." He also recommended she read particular passages from *David Copperfield*. Critics had complained that David's young and passionate love for Dora was unrealistic, but as he explained to Maria, "People ... little thought what reason I had to know it was true".

After an exchange of letters, the former sweethearts arranged to meet, but the Maria of the 1850s was a world away from the Maria of 1829. Dickens, who retained an astonishingly unrealistic view of women, was appalled to see that, like his wife, Maria was no longer the pretty, slim-waisted girl he remembered. Similarly to Catherine, she was a matronly woman whose figure had been changed by childbearing and age. He also found the flirtatious manner that had enthralled him as a young man to be, in the middle-aged Maria, silly and irritating. Dickens had begun working on *Little Dorrit* and he channelled all his disappointment and frustration into his creation of Flora Finching. When Arthur Clennam arrives back from many years overseas he is disappointed at the changes wrought in his former love: "Flora, always tall, had grown to be very broad too, and short of breath; but that was not much. Flora, whom he had left a lily, had become a peony; but that was not much. Flora, who had seemed enchanting in all she said and thought, was diffuse and silly. That was much. Flora, who had been spoiled and artless long ago, was determined to be spoiled and artless now. That was a fatal blow."

In their youth, Maria had been Dickens's superior in terms of wealth, class and sophistication. By 1855, the situation had been utterly reversed: Maria's former suitor, whom her father had scorned and she herself had teased and made miserable, was one of the most famous men in the world, with a fortune far in excess of that of either her father or her husband. This time it was Dickens who performed the rejection and Maria who was left humiliated.

In an ironic twist of fate, Maria is buried in Highland Road Cemetery in Southsea, Portsmouth – a short walk from the house in which Charles Dickens was born and very close to the grave of his mistress, Ellen Ternan.

RIGHT A painting of Maria Beadnell and her younger brother. The ambience of the portrait clearly shows how much more affluent her childhood was than that of her admirer Charles Dickens.

OPPOSITE This portrait of Dickens at the age of 18 – shortly after he met Maria Beadnell – was painted by his aunt, Janet Barrow.

THE PICKWICK PAPERS

The Posthumous Papers of the Pickwick Club, *to give its full title,*
was Dickens's first novel, published in 1836–37. It was also one of his
most lighthearted works of fiction, with a series of farcical happenings and
brilliantly created humorous characters that made the book a critical success
and set its author on the road to fame.

The germ of the idea came from Dickens's publishers, Chapman & Hall, who asked him to write a story around a series of illustrations depicting Cockney sporting events, by the artist Robert Seymour. Dickens was not keen on the pictures, so he came up with a new idea instead, based very loosely on the original suggestion, and requested that Seymour create new illustrations to go with his story. He disliked these too. Following his untimely death, Seymour was replaced first by an illustrator called Robert Buss and later by one of the most famous of Dickens's illustrators, Hablot Knight Browne, better known by the pseudonym "Phiz".

The Pickwick Papers' main characters include Samuel Pickwick, Augustus Snodgrass, Nathaniel Winkle and Tracy Tupman; the story centres on the journey of discovery the group of friends decide to undertake and their adventures along the way. Dickens took the name of Pickwick from the proprietor of a coach company in Bath, Moses Pickwick. While he was working as a journalist, Dickens often used Pickwick's coaches to travel between London and Bath. The author paid homage to

the original in chapter 35 of the novel: Mr Pickwick is travelling by stagecoach and is astonished to see on the door of the coach "in gilt letters of a goodly size ... the magic name of PICKWICK" and, as an indignant Sam Weller points out, "they put 'Moses' afore it".

The characters whom Pickwick and his friends encounter, including Sam Weller, the Wardle family, Alfred Jingle and Mrs Bardell, became instant favourites with Dickens's early readers. The commercial implications were huge, and soon, shops could be found selling merchandise such as china figurines and toby jugs of the characters, and Mr Pickwick-style spectacles and waistcoats. Sam Weller became one of the most-quoted characters in contemporary fiction and Chapman & Hall realized they had an unprecedented success on their hands. Astonishingly, Dickens had started writing *The Pickwick Papers* when he was just 24 years old.

Mr Pickwick finds himself in a number of farcical situations, including being sued for "breach of promise", but interestingly, Dickens also chose to imprison his character in a debtors' prison, a theme he would return

to many times throughout his fiction while keeping his own genuine association with the Marshalsea a deeply guarded secret. There were five debtors' prisons in London at this date; Mr Pickwick ends up not in the Marshalsea but in the Fleet prison. Dickens's younger brother Fred, who was still a teenager while his brother was writing *The Pickwick Papers*, would also end up an imprisoned debtor, incarcerated in the Queen's Bench prison.

ABOVE Dickens often used real places as inspiration for his stories; The White Hart Inn in Southwark appears prominently in *The Pickwick Papers*.

RIGHT The cover of *The Pickwick Papers* was designed by Robert Seymour shortly before the illustrator committed suicide. Dickens was still writing under the pen name Boz.

81

commanding tone.

"Sir," said the green-grocer.
"Have you got your gloves on?"
"Then Take the kiver off"

"Yes Sir."

The green grocer did as he was told with great humility, and obsequiously handed Mr Tuckle the carving knife, in doing which, he acci= dentally ~~sipped~~ sipped.

"What do you mean by that, ~~blow~~ Sir?" said Mr Tuckle, with great asperity.

"I beg your pardon Sir" — replied the crest-fallen green grocer "—I didn't mean to do it Sir; I was up very late last night Sir"

"I tell you what my opinion of you, is, Harris" — said Mr Tuckle ~~—~~ with a most impressive air "You're a ~~—~~ vulgar beast."

"I hope gentlemen "—said Harris "that you won't be ~~too hard~~ severe with me, gentlemen. I'm very much obliged to you indeed gentlemen for your patronage, and also for your recommendations gentlemen whenever additional assistance in waiting is required. ~~~~ I hope gentlemen, give satisfaction."

OPPOSITE *The Pickwick Papers* manuscript. *The Pickwick Papers* became a marketing phenomenon and turned Charles Dickens into a household name. It was printed in 20 monthly parts, beginning in relative obscurity but becoming a cult classic. Even before Dickens had finished writing the final chapters, several plagiarized adaptations had been created for the stage.

RIGHT Pickwick addresses the club, in an illustration by Seymour. Although Seymour's images became iconic, Dickens was not happy with his portrayal of the characters and worked much more closely with his later illustrators.

The Tragedy of Robert Seymour

Although Chapman & Hall deemed Robert Seymour's style the perfect complement to the work of the newly discovered Charles Dickens, Dickens was, unfortunately, not a fan of Seymour's work. In April 1836, after a meeting with Dickens in which it is possible Seymour had been told another illustrator was going to be found for *The Pickwick Papers*, the artist – who had a history of depression – went home and destroyed all his papers. He then committed suicide by shooting himself in the heart. His death was discussed in the second issue of *The Pickwick Papers*: "Before this Number reaches ... our readers, they will have become acquainted with the melancholy death of Mr Seymour, under circumstances of a very distressing nature. Some time must elapse, before the void which the deceased gentleman has left in his profession can be filled up."

6

THE HOGARTH FAMILY

On 1 June 1814, George Hogarth married Georgina Thomson in Edinburgh, Scotland. Within a year of the wedding, Georgina gave birth to their first child, Catherine Thomson Hogarth. She was born on 19 May 1815, destined to be the eldest of a family of nine children. Many days' journey away, in the southeast of England, Charles Dickens had recently celebrated his third birthday.

George and Georgina Hogarth had nine surviving children: Catherine (1815–79), Robert (1816–43), Mary (1819–37), George (1821–41), William (b. 1823), James (d. 1876), Georgina (1827–1917) and twins Helen (1833–90) and Edward (1833–79). Other Hogarth children died in infancy, but official records for that time are scarce and not all births and deaths were registered. An early report states that Georgina gave birth to 14 children; if correct, this would mean that five of her babies died.

At the time of the wedding, George was an amateur musician working as a legal writer and studying to become a lawyer. Georgina's father, George Thomson, was also a musician, as well as being a publisher and a friend of the novelist Sir Walter Scott. Through his father-in-law, George Hogarth became friendly with Scott and was employed as his legal advisor. After Scott's death, George Hogarth found it increasingly difficult to make enough money to support his family and, at the age of 47, he decided to change careers, giving up the law in favour of journalism.

The family left their native Scotland and moved to England, where George worked for a while in Exeter before moving on to Halifax in Yorkshire and the *Halifax Guardian*. In 1834, not long after Catherine's nineteenth birthday, her father accepted a post as the music critic on the *Morning Chronicle*, based in London. The family moved to Fulham, which was at that time a pretty rural area on the outskirts of London, famed for its market gardens. Within a short while, George had also been appointed editor of a sister paper, the *Evening Chronicle*.

It was during his time at the *Morning Chronicle*, in 1834, that George Hogarth first made the acquaintance of Charles Dickens, who was aged 22 and working on the articles that would form *Sketches by Boz*. Hogarth, intrigued by the young writer and convinced he would become a great success, not only took him on to write for the *Evening Chronicle*, but also invited him to his home in Fulham and introduced him to his family. Dickens was

OPPOSITE In this painting by Daniel Maclise, a young Catherine Dickens is holding an embroidered overmantel, which is presumably her own work.

MARY HOGARTH

"Kate Nickleby" and other characters

ABOVE This is the only known portrait of Mary Hogarth, who died aged 17. The original, by "Phiz", was painted after Mary's death from the artist's memory.

in turn a great admirer of Hogarth's writing and when, in 1836, Dickens became editor of the literary magazine *Bentley's Miscellany*, he commissioned his by then father-in-law to write articles. Hogarth also published a book on musical history, in 1838.

To mark his 23rd birthday, in February 1835, Dickens held a party at his chambers at Furnival's Inn, Holborn, to which he invited Catherine Hogarth. She wrote in a letter to her cousin: "it was a delightful party ... Mr Dickens improves very much on acquaintance." By the summer of that year, the couple were formally engaged; they married in 1836.

Catherine was not the only Hogarth daughter to become entranced by this enthusiastic and ambitious friend of their father's. Mary Hogarth adored – and was adored by – her brother-in-law, and stayed for long periods in the young couple's home. On the night of Saturday 6 May 1837, Dickens, Catherine and Mary returned home to Doughty Street after a night at St James's Theatre. They had been watching an operetta that Dickens had written jointly with the composer John Hullah, *The Village Coquettes*. Shortly after Mary went to bed, Charles and Catherine heard a strange cry from her room: rushing in, they found she had collapsed. A doctor was called immediately but on the following afternoon she died, in Dickens's arms; her death was believed to have been caused by a hereditary heart condition prevalent in the Hogarth family.

On hearing of her daughter's death, Mrs Hogarth went into shock and remained almost comatose for a full week. Catherine had been pregnant, and her own shock was the likely cause of her miscarriage soon after her sister's death. Dickens paid for Mary's funeral and wrote the epitaph for her gravestone: "Young, beautiful, and good, God numbered her among his angels at the early age of seventeen." Mary was buried at Kensal Green Cemetery in London. Ten days after her death, Dickens wrote to Thomas Beard: "I knew [Mary's] inmost heart, and her real worth and value. She had not a fault."

For many years, Dickens was strangely insistent that he wanted to be buried in the same plot as Mary. This was

ABOVE RIGHT This pencil drawing by Dickens's friend Daniel Maclise depicts the author with his wife Catherine and her sister Georgina. It dates from c.1843, shortly after Georgina came to live with them.

My Father as I Recall Him

In *My Father as I Recall Him*, Charles's daughter Mamie Dickens wrote about an episode during her father's courtship of Catherine:

He went one summer evening to call upon her. The Hogarths were living a little way out of London, in a residence which had a drawing-room opening with French windows onto a lawn. In this room my mother and her family were seated quietly after dinner ... when suddenly a young sailor jumped through one of the open windows into the apartment, whistled and danced a hornpipe, and before they could recover from their amazement jumped out again. A few minutes later my father walked in at the door as sedately as though quite innocent of the prank, and shook hands with everyone.

one of the peculiarities of his behaviour, along with the wearing of her ring on his little finger, for the rest of his life, which led to rumours that he and Mary had been having an affair. When Mary was alive, Dickens's writing about her suggests his feelings were purely fraternal; it was only after her death that he began writing as if he had been in love with her. It seems that the shock of Mary's death prompted the first recorded instance of Dickens's severe depressions, although his novels, particularly *David Copperfield*, suggest this was a condition that had plagued him since childhood. Mary's death affected him grievously and the shock never seemed completely to dissipate. After Mary and Catherine's brother George died in 1841, Dickens was forced to concede that George should be buried in Mary's grave instead of him, but wrote to John Forster, "I cannot bear the thought of being excluded from her dust".

A few years after Mary's death, her younger sister Georgina went to live with the Dickens family. She was there, primarily, to help Catherine with the children, but Georgina and Charles shared an intense friendship, and many people believed they were lovers. Rumours of an affair persist even today, prompting a DNA test to be carried out by a man in Argentina convinced he was descended from Dickens and Georgina. The test proved he had no DNA connection to the Dickens or Hogarth families. It is likely that Georgina was in love with Charles – she certainly had no other love affair and refused offers of marriage – but it is extremely unlikely that her romantic feelings were reciprocated. She did, however, supersede Catherine in Charles's affections: he was in awe of the way Georgina managed the household and children, and her obvious capabilities – unhindered by the constant pregnancies and childbirths experienced by Catherine – caused a deep rift between the sisters. When, in 1858, Charles humiliated Catherine by insisting on a separation, Georgina, highly critical of her sister, took Charles's side and remained living with him and the children. It was her family who began the rumours that Georgina was Dickens's mistress, something which so enraged the author that he arranged for Georgina to have a "virginity test". The deeply humiliating medical

RIGHT Collins's Farm in Hampstead, where the Dickens family took a recuperative holiday following the sudden death of Mary Hogarth in 1837. Then a rural haven, it is now part of north London.

assessment was carried out by a male doctor and must have been excruciating for Georgina. The certificate of virginity was obtained and Georgina never forgave her family for her humiliation, just as they never forgave her for her part in Catherine's downfall. Georgina lost her parents and her siblings, but retained the love and respect of her sister's husband and children. Dickens described Georgina as "the best and truest friend [a] man ever had".

BELOW Georgina Hogarth remained loyal to her brother-in-law through thick and thin. Her decision to stay with Dickens after his separation from Catherine meant she was shunned by her family.

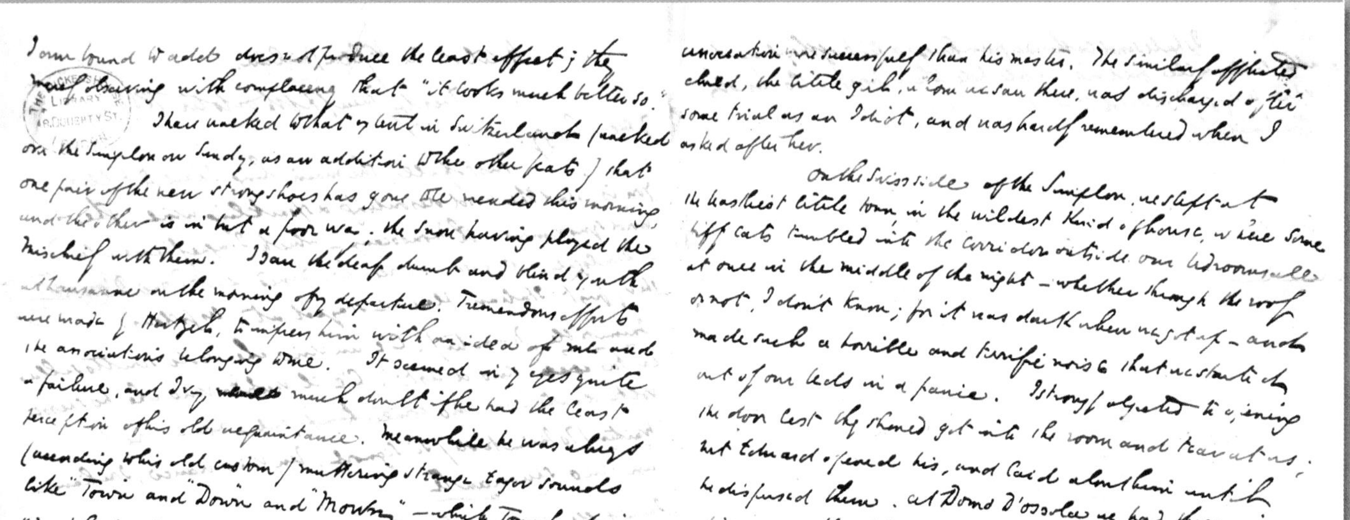
Town bound to add it doesn't produce the least effect; the
[illegible] observing with complacency that "it looks much better so."
I have asked what my boots in Switzerland (walked over the Simplon on Sunday, as an addition to the other feats) that one pair of the new strong shoes has gone to be mended this morning and the other is in but a poor way. The snow having played the mischief with them. I saw the deaf dumb and blind youth at Lausanne on the morning of my departure. Tremendous efforts were made by Hertzel, to impress him with an idea of me and the associations belonging to me. It seemed in my eyes quite a failure, and I very much doubt if he had the least perception of his old acquaintance. Meanwhile he was always (according to his old custom) muttering strange eager sounds like "Town and "Down and "Mouth" — which Townshend, in a most ludicrous manner, insisted into an irrepressible desire on the poor fellow's part to articulate his name. As he evidently had no more idea of Townshend than of any lamp post in London it was so extraordinarily absurd that I laughed disgracefully and could not be stopped. The interview terminated by Townshend's laying my object down in that dismal little place where we used to see the boy at work — he perpetually coming back again for that purpose (when we were wild to get away, lest we should lose the boat) and saying, in the oddest French "combien cette chose là? — Oh! — Voulez-vous donc avoir la bonté d'envoyer cet objet chez — moi? Et cet autre objet — combien? — Oh! — Vrai-ment! — Voulez-vous donc envoyer — cet objet — aussi — chez moi — Bon soir." We forced him out at last, and I left ten francs to be spent in cigars for my old friend. If I had taken one with me, I think I must have established the communication more successfully than his master. The similarly afflicted child, the little girl, whom we saw there, was discharged after some trial as an Idiot, and was hardly remembered when I asked after her.

On the Swiss side of the Simplon, we slept at the nastiest little town in the wildest kind of house, where some tiff cats tumbled into the corridor outside our bedrooms all at once in the middle of the night — whether through the roof or not, I don't know; for it was dark when we got up — and made such a horrible and terrific noise that we started up out of our beds in a panic. I strongly objected to opening the door lest they should get into the room and tear at us; but Edward opened his, and laid about him until he dispersed them. At Domo d'Ossola we had three immense bedrooms (Egg's bed twelve feet wide!) and a Sala of imperceptible extent in the dim light of two candles and a wood fire; but were very well and very cheaply entertained. Here we are, as you know, housed in the greatest comfort.

We continue to get on very well indeed together, though I am rather confirmed in general suspicions I have long entertained that other men in general (and Collins in particular) spit and snort rather more than I have ever found it necessary to do — particularly in the early part of the day. We really do admirably. I lose no opportunity of inculcating the lesson that it is of no use to be out of temper in travelling, and it is very seldom wanted for any of us. Egg is an excellent fellow and full of good qualities — I am sure a generous and staunch man at heart. He is not above the average, intellectually; but I believe he is, in a good and honourable nature.

OPPOSITE & ABOVE Letter to Georgina Hogarth,
25 October 1853.

7

MARRIED LIFE

On 2 April 1836, shortly after the publication of the first part of
The Pickwick Papers, *Charles Dickens and Catherine Hogarth were*
married in London, at the newly built St Luke's church in Chelsea.
Although Dickens claimed in later life he had never been in love
with Catherine and the marriage was a mistake from the start,
his letters to her belie that.

During their engagement he wrote to her of his longing for them to live together and of wanting "to turn round to you at our own fireside when my work is done and seek in your kind looks and gentle manner the recreation and happiness which the moping solitude of chambers can never afford". Dickens also confided to Catherine the story of his impecunious childhood and the humiliation it had brought him. Even most of his closest friends learned about this only after Dickens's death, when John Forster published his biography and revealed his friend's carefully guarded secret.

At the start of their marriage, Charles and Catherine Dickens lived in what had been his bachelor quarters, at Furnival's Inn in the London legal district in Holborn. Charles's younger brother Fred remained with them, and the small apartment must have been rather crowded since – as was common practice at the time – Catherine's sister Mary effectively moved in too. After a prolonged stay at this first home, she wrote to a friend of her "delightfully happy month with dearest Catherine in her own house ... she makes a most capital housekeeper and is as happy

as the day is long – I think they are more devoted than ever since their marriage."

The couple's first baby, Charles Dickens Junior, was born at Furnival's Inn, but babies and children were not allowed to live in the building and the family needed to move. In their new home, at 48 Doughty Street in Bloomsbury, Fred had a room in the attic, close to the children and the servants, while Mary, who continued to stay with them regularly, slept in the bedroom next to that of Charles and Catherine. Many books have suggested Dickens had an affair with his wife's young sister, but that seems both unlikely and unrealistic. Catherine adored her closest sister and does not seem to have resented her presence in their home (as she would later resent that of her sister Georgina); instead she valued

OPPOSITE This portrait of Charles, and its companion overleaf of Catherine, are by Samuel Laurence (1812–84). The artist had many literary friends and began his own club, the Bohemian Phalanstery.

William, by Divine Providence, Archbishop of CANTERBURY,

Primate of all ENGLAND and Metropolitan. To our well-beloved in CHRIST,

Charles Dickens of Furnivals Inn

in the County of Middlesex Bachelor and

Catherine Hogarth of the Parish of

Saint Luke Chelsea in the same County

of Minister a Minor

GRACE and HEALTH. **WHEREAS** ye are, as it is alledged, resolved to proceed to the Solemnization of true and lawful Matrimony

with the consent of George Hogarth the natural and lawful

Father of the said Minor

and that you greatly desire that the same may be solemnized in the Face of the Church: We being willing that these your honest Desires may the more speedily obtain a due Effect, and to the end therefore that this Marriage may be publicly and lawfully solemnized in the Parish Church of

Saint Luke Chelsea aforesaid

by the RECTOR, VICAR, or CURATE thereof, without the Publication or Proclamation of the Banns of Matrimony, provided there shall appear no Impediment of Kindred or Alliance, or of any other lawful Cause, nor any Suit commenced in any Ecclesiastical Court, to bar or hinder the Proceeding of the said Matrimony, according to the Tenor of this Licence : And likewise, That the Celebration of this Marriage be had and done publicly in ———— the aforesaid Church ———— between the Hours of Eight and Twelve in the Forenoon. We, for lawful Causes, graciously grant this our **Licence and Faculty,** as well to you the Parties contracting, as to the RECTOR, VICAR, CURATE, or MINISTER, of ———— the aforesaid Parish ———— who is designed to solemnize the Marriage between you, in the Manner and Form above specified, according to the Rites of the Book of Common Prayer, set forth for that Purpose, by the Authority of Parliament. **Given** under the Seal of our **Vicar General** this *Twenty ninth* Day of *March* ———— in the Year of our Lord One Thousand Eight Hundred and Thirty-six, and in the Eighth Year of our Translation.

John Moore

Registrar

Mary's advice and assistance, particularly the help Mary provided to a post-natally depressed Catherine following the birth of her first child.

While living at Doughty Street, after Mary's death, Catherine gave birth to her two eldest daughters: Mary, known as "Mamie", who was named after her beloved aunt, and Katey (Catherine), named after her mother. At this time in their marriage, Charles and Catherine were happy and seemingly well matched. They shared an enthusiasm for life, a love of parties and socializing, and a love of dancing.

In 1842, Catherine accompanied Charles on a trip to America that lasted nearly six months, leaving the children at home, although their fourth child was only 11 months old. When they set sail, they asked Catherine's 15-year-old sister Georgina to visit the four children as often as possible. "Aunty Georgy" became a great favourite with the children and, shortly after Charles and Catherine's return to England, she was asked to move in with the family permanently. Initially, Georgina's presence in the house and the family was welcomed by Catherine; it would be some time before she came to regret allowing her sister to take such a prominent role in her marriage.

After 15 years of pregnancy and child rearing, Catherine was no longer the vivacious, pretty, wasp-waisted girl Charles Dickens had fallen in love with. She was worn down by constant childbearing, having given birth to 10 children and suffered at least two miscarriages. Although her condition was not understood at the time, it is apparent today – through letters and diaries – that Catherine also suffered from regular and deeply debilitating post-natal depression. It seems she experienced it every time she gave birth, as well as suffering grief from her miscarriages and the death of baby Dora. As one who also suffered from depression, Charles was initially understanding. Mental health was little understood in Victorian England, but in the early years of their marriage, he attempted to find a cure for Catherine's depressions, such as taking her to

RIGHT Catherine Dickens by Samuel Laurence.

OPPOSITE Marriage Certificate. This facsimile of Charles Dickens and Catherine Hogarth's marriage certificate records their wedding at St Luke's Church in Chelsea, London, on 2 April 1836. Later that year, a new rector arrived at the church. His name was Reverend Charles Kingsley; his son, also named Charles, was the author of *The Water Babies*.

What Shall We Have for Dinner?

In 1852, Catherine published a book, *What Shall We Have for Dinner?*. The cookbook, which provided recipes for up to 18 guests, was published under the pseudonym Lady Maria Clutterbuck (one of the amateur theatrical roles she had played). More than simply a recipe book, it was a guide for young wives bewildered by finding themselves in charge of their own homes for the first time – Catherine's book appeared several years before Mrs Beeton published her famous *Book of Household Management*. Several misogynist critics have claimed the book was written by Charles Dickens, refusing to permit Catherine the ability to write a book of her own (and never pausing to wonder why on earth Dickens would have made the time in his busy schedule to write it and then disclaim it). *What Shall We Have for Dinner?* was regularly updated and republished until 1860.

ABOVE The newlywed Mr and Mrs Dickens spent their honeymoon here, in the village of Chalk in Kent. The following year they returned to Chalk with their baby son, Charley.

Malvern for the water cure and learning to use mesmerism, a form of hypnosis, which he practised on her. As their family grew, however, Charles seemed to blame Catherine for the ever-increasing number of children he needed to provide for. In a letter written after the initial joy of becoming a father had begun to wear thin, he described his pregnant wife as being in "that uninteresting condition".

There was a much more vital and amusing side to Catherine than her husband's later accounts ever do justice to. She was a witty and kind hostess with an ability to put adults and children at their ease. William Thackeray's two motherless daughters remembered her with great fondness. Anny, the elder of the two, particularly remembered attending a children's party at the Dickenses' home, when Catherine complimented the nervous little girls' dresses and found them dancing partners.

Catherine continued to adore her husband – her remaining letters suggest perhaps to the point of hero-worship – and as the marriage grew older she was to be continually disappointed by his inability to reciprocate her feelings. She has long been memorialized and remembered purely in terms of being the wife of Charles Dickens, and her memory has been blighted by untrue accusations. One of the most persistent whispers was that she was an alcoholic – a baseless rumour that seems to have been started by fans of Dickens who were trying to justify the author's abandonment of his wife.

By the mid-1850s, the marriage was in serious trouble. Charles was bored and lonely in a marriage that had come to feel like a prison, and had begun to crave excitement; Catherine was bewildered and scared at the changes that had taken place not only in their marriage but in her husband's career and personality. She had married a man who was inferior to her in social and financial status but over the years had seen him develop into a celebrity so universally adored that he now seemed to have been placed far outside the necessarily small, domestic world that Catherine inhabited. With Georgina Hogarth caught in the middle, the situation was a dangerous one that was about to ignite.

ABOVE The Dickens family lived at 48 Doughty Street, Bloomsbury, for two years. Today this house is the Charles Dickens Museum – the only one of Dickens's London homes to have survived.

8

THE TEN DICKENS CHILDREN

Charles and Catherine Dickens's first child was Charles Dickens Junior ("Charley"), who was born nine months and four days after his parents' marriage.

Charley's birthday was 6 January 1857, on Twelfth Night, a popular holiday in Victorian England. Throughout his childhood, his birthday was celebrated in boisterous style, with Twelfth Night parties, cake and dancing. As the family increased and the children became old enough to act on stage, Charley's birthday became the date on which the family theatricals would be performed.

There were ten children born to Charles and Catherine Dickens: seven boys and three girls. The youngest daughter, Dora, died in infancy, but the remaining nine all survived to adulthood. Losing one child out of ten was not unusual; in nineteenth-century England, one in five died before their fifth birthday (in the poorest parts of London, this statistic rose to one in three). Of the seven Dickens sons, five were sent to live overseas; only Charley and Henry remained living in England.

Catherine Dickens spent much of her life pregnant, or recovering from a birth or miscarriage. She also suffered from depression, and her children were largely looked after by servants and by Catherine's younger sister, Georgina. As the children grew up, Catherine played an increasingly marginalized role. She was seldom consulted by her husband

in decisions made about the children's lives and was unable to prevent her five sons being sent abroad, although she was desperately unhappy at the thought of their leaving.

Today, Victorian fathers have a reputation for having been distant and unloving. Charles Dickens, however, was actively involved with his children's upbringing and loved being a father, although he found the quieter girls easier to cope with than the rowdy boys. Katey is usually referred to – by her siblings as well as historians – as his favourite child, apart from a period of several years when she was usurped by the baby of the family, Edward (nicknamed "Plornishmaroontigoonter" and always known as "Plorn"). Dickens loved babies, but he found their passage through childhood and adolescence somewhat bewildering, and often dreaded the disruption to his writing routine caused by his sons coming home for school holidays. In many of his letters, he writes cynically to friends about the irritation of having an ever-increasing family – he famously attributed Catherine's continual pregnancies to her own "perversity" in getting herself pregnant – yet he remained a loving and indulgent father in private.

ABOVE LEFT Charley (1837–96), whose full name was Charles Culliford Boz Dickens. The name Culliford came from his maternal grandmother, Mary. Boz was in honour of his father's pseudonym – famous by the time of Charley's birth.

ABOVE RIGHT Mamie Dickens (1838–96) photographed with her dog, a white Pomeranian named Mrs Bouncer. Mamie recalled in her book about her father that Mrs Bouncer was "a special gift to me".

Marriages and Children

Charley married his childhood sweetheart, Bessie Evans, the daughter of one of Dickens's publishers (Frederick Evans of Bradbury & Evans). When Dickens fell out with Bradbury & Evans, at around the time he separated from his wife, he became fiercely opposed to his son's choice of wife and refused to attend the wedding, insisting the marriage wouldn't last. Despite those prophecies, Charley and Bessie remained happily married and had eight children: seven daughters and one son. Their eldest child, Mary Angela Dickens, became a prolific and well-respected novelist. The only boy in the family, Charles Walter Dickens, ran away with a barmaid, whom he married, and was disowned by his parents.

Despite receiving at least two proposals of marriage, Mamie chose not to marry and had no children; nor did Walter, Frank or Sydney.

Katey married twice: her first husband was the Pre-Raphaelite artist Charles ("Charlie") Allston Collins, younger brother of the novelist Wilkie Collins. The marriage appears to have been unconsummated; Charlie was possibly impotent and probably homosexual. Katey had at least one affair, with the artist Valentine Prinsep, but she and Charlie remained close and she nursed him through terminal stomach cancer. Shortly after being widowed in 1873, she married an Italian-born artist, Carlo Perugini. They had one child, a son named Leonard Ralph

Dickens Perugini ("Dickie"). Tragically, he died aged just seven months and they had no more children.

Alfred married Jessie (née Devlin) in 1873; it was a happy marriage and they had two daughters. In 1878, Jessie was travelling in a carriage that overturned, was thrown from her seat and died soon afterwards from head injuries. Ten years later, Alfred married again. His second wife, Emile (née Riley), was 19 years his junior; the marriage was not as happy as his first and they had no children. Neither of Alfred's daughters married or had children.

Henry's wife was Marie (née Roche), a French-speaking Catholic – her religion, in which faith all their children were baptized, caused a certain amount of consternation within the family. They had a very happy marriage which produced seven children: three daughters and four sons. One of their sons, Gerald, became an admiral in the Royal Navy. One of their daughters, Elaine, always known in the family as "Bobby", lived to the age of 95. The youngest of the children, Cedric, was killed during the Battle of the Somme. One of Henry and Marie's many grandchildren

was the novelist Monica Dickens.

Plorn (Edward) got married in Australia, to the aptly named Constance (née Desailly), the daughter of a sheep farmer and one of the first generation of women in Australia to learn the new skill of typing. The couple had no children and their life together was often difficult, as Plorn fell regularly into debt. Towards the end of his life, they were living in extreme poverty; his siblings Katey and Henry sent him money, but the postal service took so long that the money arrived too late. Constance nursed Plorn tirelessly until the end.

Careers

After leaving school, Charley went to study in Germany, a popular destination for boys destined for the business world. He then worked for Barings Bank, in the City of London, before going to Hong Kong to learn about the tea trade. In the late 1860s, he set up his own business in the paper industry; it failed and Charley was declared bankrupt. Although estranged from his father, he turned to

RIGHT This portrait of Katey (1839–1929) was painted by her second husband, Carlo Perugini, following their official marriage in 1874. He painted roses in her cap because they were her favourite flower.

OPPOSITE LEFT Walter Dickens (1841–63), photographed before he left England in 1857 to travel to India as a cadet in the East India Company. He would be promoted to the rank of lieutenant in the 42nd Highlanders.

OPPOSITE RIGHT Frank Dickens (1844–86) initially wanted to be a doctor, but ended up a hero of the Royal Canadian Mounted Police.

him for help: the rift was healed and Charley became editor of *All the Year Round*, a magazine Charles had founded. After Charles Dickens's death, Charley tried to continue with the magazine, but it was the author's celebrity that had ensured its popularity; once again, Charley found himself in financial trouble, and in poor health. He died at the age of 59 and is buried in Mortlake, south London.

Mamie became her father's housekeeper until the end of his life and a local celebrity in Kent, renowned for being the first woman seen riding a bicycle. In 1867, she was asked to christen and launch a new ship at the Chatham docks, where her grandfather had once worked. After the

death of her father, Mamie seems to have embarrassed or angered most of her siblings, and much of her life post-1870 remains shrouded in mystery. She is known to have spent some years living with a progressive clergyman and his wife in the suburbs of Manchester, a circumstance which reputedly caused a "scandal", hushed up by her family. Mamie also wrote a book, *My Father as I Recall Him* (in which she barely mentions her mother). She died on the day of her brother Charley's funeral and is buried in Sevenoaks, Kent, beside Katey and her family.

Katey became a respected professional artist, renowned for her portraits of children; her work continues to sell at

BY 7.0.3.0.

OF GAR (19)

Acc 0326 BY 3.0.R.6.

BY 7.0.R.6

Garibaldi

LEFT This photo album
was owned by Katey
Dickens, and contains
intimate portraits of the
family and their pets.
Katey was born in 1839,
the same year in which
the first daguerreotype
was invented. As an
artist, she found the
art of photography
enthralling.

FAR LEFT Alfred Dickens (1845–1912) was fortunate in his parents' choice of godfathers: Count Alfred d'Orsay and Alfred, Lord Tennyson, soon to be named poet laureate. In this photograph, one can see that he has inherited his father's love of fashionable clothes.

LEFT Edward (1852–1902), always known as "Plorn", photographed at the age of 16 before his departure for Australia. The gun was his father's farewell present. The dark circles under his eyes suggest Plorn's deep unhappiness at being sent away. His life in Australia was difficult and he was never truly happy.

BELOW Sydney Dickens (1845–72) in his naval cadet uniform. He joined the navy at the age of 13, setting sail for Canada when he was just 14 years old. His father's early pride turned to shame as Sydney fell into terrible debt and became notorious in the navy for his "dissolute" lifestyle.

auction today. During her first marriage, she produced little of import (and very little work from this time remains in existence), but during her second marriage her artistic output flourished. In 1877, she was accepted to exhibit at the Royal Academy in London – a feat few women of her era achieved. Katey was also an occasional artist's model, for John Everett Millais (most famously in his 1860 painting *The Black Brunswicker*) as well as for her husbands. She died four months before her 90th birthday and is buried with her second husband and their baby in Sevenoaks, Kent.

As a teenager, Walter was accepted by the East India Company as a cadet. He left England with the 26th Native Infantry Regiment at the age of 16 and would later become a lieutenant in the 42nd Highlanders (better known as the Black Watch). The year he arrived in India was 1857 – an inauspicious time to begin his career, as it marked the start of the so-called 'Indian Mutiny'. Walter was popular among his peers, but his parents and siblings became increasingly frustrated by his behaviour as he fell regularly into deep debt. After paying his son's debts several times, Charles Dickens wrote and told Walter he would not bail him out any more as it was unfair to his other children. A few months later, Walter was on his way home on sick leave and hoping to heal the rift with his father when he died very suddenly from an aneurysm. He was only 22 years old. He is buried in Calcutta (present-day Kolkata).

Frank was originally destined to be a doctor, but a series of health problems in his teens affected his education and he was unable to pass the required exams. After leaving school he worked with his father, briefly, on *All the Year Round,* before travelling to India and beginning a career in the Bengal Mounted Police. He arrived in India to the news that his brother Walter had died. In 1874, Frank moved to Canada and became one of the first officers in the Royal Canadian Mounted Police; he was hailed as a hero during the wars between the new settlers and the First Nations. In 1886, Frank went to the USA to give a lecture and died of a sudden heart attack. He is buried in Moline, Illinois.

Alfred had wanted to go into the army, but failed the entrance exam. He worked in London for two years in a "China house", a company trading with the Far East, before moving to Australia at the age of 19. He took after his father in his love of fashionable clothes and, before leaving England, ran up several debts, in his father's name, mostly in tailors' bills. Charles Dickens bought Alfred a sheep farm in Australia, in which venture Alfred was later joined by his youngest brother, Plorn. After a fierce drought left the business in ruins, Alfred left farming to become a respected businessman. In later life, he gave lecture tours about his father, returning to England for the first time in 1910. In 1912, he travelled to the USA. He died unexpectedly in New York while on a lecture tour and is buried there.

In 1860, at the age of 13, Sydney became a cadet at the naval school in Portsmouth. The following year, he joined his first ship, *HMS Orlando*, and sailed for Halifax; in 1867, he proudly told his family that he had been promoted to the rank of lieutenant. Despite this promising start, Sydney was to fall heavily into debt, resulting in trouble not only with his family but also with the navy. He became increasingly dissolute and his health began to fail. Two weeks after his 25th birthday, while on his way home on sick leave, he died on board the hospital ship. His childhood nickname of "Ocean Spectre" became chillingly apt, as he was buried at sea in the Indian Ocean.

Henry left Cambridge with a good law degree and became a barrister. A popular figure in the courts, he was later appointed a judge, became a KC and was awarded the honoured position of Common Serjeant of the City of London, from 1917 until 1932. He was knighted by King George V in 1922. Henry also gave readings, emulating the style of Charles Dickens, and wrote two books, the most popular being *Memories of My Father*. The last surviving Dickens child, Henry died in 1933 at the age of 84, after being hit by a motorcycle while crossing a road. He is buried in Putney Vale, south London.

At the age of just 16, Plorn was sent off to Australia to join Alfred. He had been prepared for his career as a sheep farmer by studying at Cirencester Agricultural College. When the sheep farm failed, the two brothers ran a stock and station agency, although they later stopped working together. While Alfred created a successful career, Plorn was not as successful. It seems he harboured a huge resentment against his family in England about being sent away at such a young age, and fell into debt on numerous occasions, which he expected his siblings to

pay off. In 1889 he was elected MP for Wincannia in New South Wales, a post he held for five years. He fell into debt again soon afterwards, however, and his health began to fail. He died in Moree, NSW, and is buried there.

RIGHT Henry Dickens (1849–1933) was the only one of the siblings to go to university. Later, he wrote two non-fiction books: *Memories of My Father* and *Recollections of Sir Henry Fielding Dickens KC*.

OLIVER TWIST

After the jollity of The Pickwick Papers, *Dickens's second novel (published in 1837–39) broke surprising new ground. Its focus on social injustice and attack on civil institutions – such as the workhouses, the New Poor Law and a legal system that allowed children to be sold like slaves – made him a champion of the people.*

The novel's full title, *The Adventures of Oliver Twist, or, The Parish Boy's Progress*, identifies Oliver with the saintly hero of John Bunyan's *The Pilgrim's Progress* (1678).

Dickens's workload was both exhilarating and exhausting, as he was working on *Oliver Twist* at the same time as he was finishing *The Pickwick Papers*. Following the death of Mary Hogarth, however, he was unable to keep working; he needed a complete break and he stopped writing both novels, explaining to his readers why there would be no instalment that month. *Oliver Twist* was originally published in *Bentley's Miscellany*, a literary magazine set up by the publisher Richard Bentley, but Dickens and Bentley had a stormy relationship and Dickens was unhappy with the way Bentley treated him. In 1839, Dickens bought all rights to *Oliver* from the publisher, paying £2,250 – the money had been provided by Chapman & Hall, his new publisher.

At the start of the novel, a heavily pregnant young woman arrives at a workhouse. She gives birth to a son, then dies; the workhouse authorities name the baby Oliver Twist. When he is nine years old, Oliver is put to work to earn his meagre keep. After getting into trouble with

the workhouse authorities, he is sold to an undertaker as an apprentice, but when he is mistreated, he runs away. He walks for days, ending up in London, where he meets "as roystering and swaggering a young gentleman as ever stood four feet six, or something less". This "strange boy" is Jack Dawkins, known to his friends as the Artful Dodger. The Dodger takes Oliver back to his home, where a gang of boys live, sleep and learn the art of thieving, all for the benefit of the aged miser Fagin.

Oliver Twist is a fast-paced adventure story in which Oliver is propelled into and out of many different worlds, which are alternately bewildering, wonderful and terrifying. The characters he encounters include kindly Mr Brownlow, vicious Bill Sikes, the abusive – and abused – Noah Claypole, gentle Rose Maylie and the sinister Monks. Although Dickens's criminal villains are as bad as he can make them, he deliberately blurs the line

OPPOSITE This is the preliminary drawing by George Cruikshank for the title page of *Oliver Twist*. His final version was turned into a woodcut. The pictures around the edge show scenes from the novel.

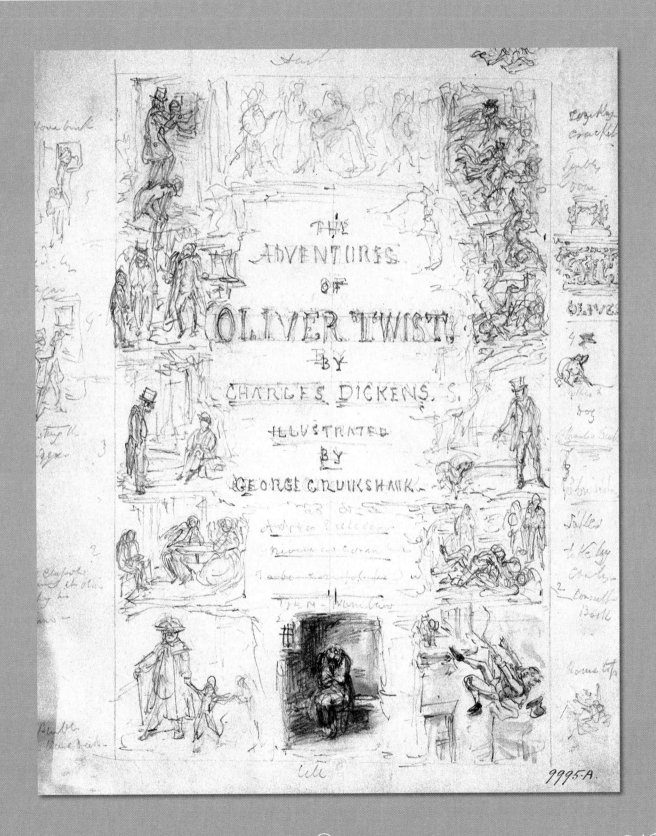

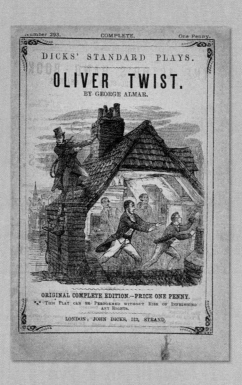

LEFT Dicks' Standard Plays were unauthorized stage adaptations of famous book, very popular with amateur actors.

BELOW This manuscript page from *Oliver Twist* shows marked differences from some of his later manuscripts. Some of the changes can be attributed to the author trying out new quill pens, using different inks and changing the types of paper he used. His handwriting also changed, however, seemingly reflecting the author's state of mind at certain stages of his life.

OPPOSITE One of Dickens's childhood homes was a few yards from the workhouse on Cleveland Street, in central London. The building was one of his inspirations when writing *Oliver Twist*.

between respectability and criminality: Mr Bumble, the parish beadle, Mrs Corney, the workhouse matron, and the "members of the board" – well-fed, wealthy men to whom the futures of the weak, infirm and poor inmates of the workhouse have been entrusted – are as abusive and uncaring as Fagin, Sikes and Monks. Fagin may teach the boys to thieve and help bring about Nancy's murder, but at least he gives the boys a warm place to sleep and plentiful food – neither of which had been given to Oliver in the workhouse, where the board had intended to sell him to a chimney sweep already responsible for the deaths of several children. Dickens's relationship with Fagin is a complicated one: he portrays his villain as unscrupulous and deeply unattractive, yet also has great compassion for Fagin as he awaits his death by hanging in the condemned cell of Newgate Prison.

Thanks to numerous successful adaptations for the stage, television and cinema, *Oliver Twist* has become one of Dickens's best-known and most iconic novels, and characters such as Fagin, Nancy, the Artful Dodger and Oliver himself remain household names.

The Queen and the Pauper

Lord Melbourne, who was prime minister when the young Princess Victoria became queen, advised his new monarch not to read *Oliver Twist* because it contained "paupers, criminals and other unpleasant subjects". In most circumstances, the Queen was swayed by Melbourne, but in this she ignored her mentor's advice. She read the novel, was said to have found it "excessively interesting" and was intrigued to meet its author. It was not until March 1870, however, that the two great figures of Victorian history had their first and only private meeting. The author died three months later.

10

NICHOLAS NICKLEBY

For many years, Dickens had heard rumours of terrible schools in
Yorkshire. In Nicholas Nickleby *he set out to try and make a change*
in British society. His third novel, published in instalments in 1838–39,
tells the story of the widowed Mrs Nickleby and her teenaged children,
Nicholas and Kate.

Finances force them to move to London and throw themselves on the mercy of Ralph Nickleby, an unpleasant moneylender irritated by the prospect of taking on his dead brother's family. Kate finds work with a dressmaker in London, but Nicholas is parcelled off to Yorkshire to become an assistant schoolmaster at Dotheboys Hall, run by the sinister and brutal Mr Wackford Squeers.

"Mr Squeers is the representative of a class, and not of an individual," wrote Dickens after *Nicholas Nickleby* was published, yet the inspiration for Wackford Squeers has long been believed to have come from his encounter with Mr William Shaw of Shaw's Academy. In his time as a court reporter, Dickens had heard rumours about Shaw, a notorious schoolmaster who had been prosecuted in the 1820s after several of his pupils had gone blind. In February 1838, Dickens went to Barnard Castle in Yorkshire, with his illustrator Phiz, to investigate the Yorkshire schools and meet Shaw. It was in the Barnard Castle churchyard that he was inspired to create one of his most tragic characters, Smike; the vision of the cruelly abused and neglected boy came to him as he gazed at the gravestone of George Ashton

Taylor, a boy who had died at Shaw's Academy.

Shaw's descendants dispute that Shaw was the cruel figure history has labelled him as. He remains, however, inextricably linked with Dickens's portrayal of Wackford Squeers (the two men share the same initials, ran their own schools and were physically similar, including the detail that both wore an eye patch). Many of Dickens's letters from the period have been lost, but one of his correspondents later claimed he had written in a letter to her that Squeers was based on Shaw. Despite this, there were several other schoolmasters who claimed the dubious honour for themselves; reputedly, at least one threatened to sue Dickens for libel and others wanted to travel to London and beat the author in the same manner in which Nicholas had beaten Squeers. Dickens later stated that "Mr Squeers and his school are faint and feeble pictures of an existing reality" – the whole truth was too harsh and miserable for him to inflict on his readers.

Nicholas Nickleby was one of Dickens's greatest social triumphs. The public began to ask whether these schools really existed, and journalists began descending on

Yorkshire. It was claimed that within two years of the novel's publication, almost all the schools had been closed down. In his preface, Dickens wrote, "The story was begun a few months after the publication of the completed *The Pickwick Papers*. There were, then, a good many cheap Yorkshire schools in existence. There are very few now."

The novel also focuses on another of Dickens's passions, the theatre. After Nicholas prevents Squeers from inflicting a brutal punishment on the boys – a punishment Nicholas metes out to Squeers instead – he flees Yorkshire. He and Smike join a theatrical company run by Mr Vincent Crummles. The ensuing episodes allowed the author to give free reign to his theatrical imagination, conjuring up unforgettable characters, including the "infant phenomenon", Miss Ninetta Crummles. This young woman, expected to remain ten years old forever, is a superb example of Dickens's ability. The situation is ludicrous and funny, and he makes his readers laugh – but underneath is a pathetic and melancholy truth: "The infant phenomenon, though short of stature, had a comparatively aged countenance, and had moreover been precisely the same age ... certainly for five good years. But she had been kept up late and put upon an unlimited allowance of gin-and-water from infancy to prevent her growing tall."

Nicholas Nickleby placed Dickens at the height of Victorian society. *The Pickwick Papers* had established him as an exciting new author and *Oliver Twist* had captured the imagination of a mass readership, but it was *Nicholas Nickleby* that truly brought him fame. From 1839 onwards, Charles Dickens was a household name.

BELOW *Theatrical emotion of Mr Vincent Crummles* by Phiz, shows the provincial actor-manager embracing an astonished Nicholas. Mr Crummles is depicted as larger than life to portray his dramatic personality.

11

THE OLD CURIOSITY SHOP

Dickens's next novel, The Old Curiosity Shop *(published in 1840–41),
grew out of a vision of writing a short story about a young girl forced to
make her way through a world of uncaring adults.*

The girl who plagued his imagination, who "followed him about everywhere", grew into Little Nell; she would become one of his best-known characters.

Nell Trent lives with her grandfather, a gambling addict and the proprietor of the Old Curiosity Shop. Her parents are dead, but she has a brother, Fred. He is bitterly jealous of his sister and convinced their grandfather has plenty of money which Nell will inherit. Despite his grandfather's insistence that there is no money, Fred is deafened by his avaricious fury and incensed at the thought of his sister being favoured over him. The biggest villain in the book, however, is Daniel Quilp, "An elderly man of remarkably hard features and forbidding aspect, and so low in stature as to be quite a dwarf, though his head and face were large enough for the body of a giant. His black eyes were relentless, sly, and cunning."

Quilp is one of Dickens's most frightening villains, a cruel, grasping, vindictive moneylender whose greatest delight in life is to make others suffer and watch their downfall. He lusts after Little Nell (who is a child, not a woman), takes sadistic pleasure in the financial ruin of his

clients, and beats his timid, downtrodden wife. Dickens's disgust for the wife-beating, paedophiliac character of his creation is apparent throughout the book and in his sympathy for Quilp's wife, "pretty little, mild-spoken" Betsey, who "performed a sound practical penance for her folly [of marrying Quilp] every day of her life".

In his preface, Dickens wrote of his desire to "surround the lonely figure of the child with grotesque and wild, but not impossible companions". His creation of Quilp, a dwarf who eats hard-boiled eggs without removing the shells and drinks boiling tea without flinching, has more in common with the fairy stories of the Brothers Grimm than with the traditions of Victorian novel-writing.

Tricked and terrorized by Quilp, the grandfather seems on the verge of insanity. He persuades Little Nell that their only option is to escape in secrecy and get as far away as possible. So the two, bound by the infirmity of age and the physical limitations of impoverished childhood, set off on their fatal journey. The journey and the people they encounter along the way allowed Dickens to give full rein to his imagination and his humour, but when Nell's health

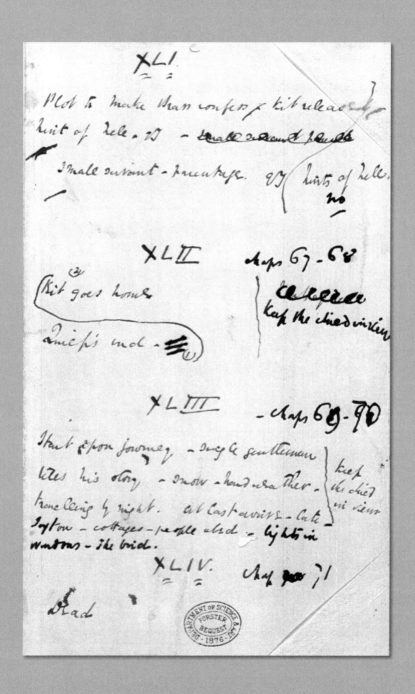

ABOVE These notes show how Dickens plotted his chapters: he simply wrote a number and a few brief jottings. He rarely wrote extensive plans, keeping most of his ideas in his head.

began failing, his readers began to realize that the author might not have a happy ending in mind. Numerous letters begged Dickens to let Little Nell live. The author, however, was suffering deeply from the process of writing the novel; there were even rumours being whispered around London that he had gone mad. The story had opened up the old wound of Mary Hogarth's death and he grieved for Little Nell as he had for his sister-in-law. He felt that the world was too cruel to allow someone as perfectly good as Little Nell to be able to live in it and he had no choice but to kill her. As he wrote to the book's illustrator, George Cattermole, "I am breaking my heart over this story." After writing the death scene, Dickens recorded, "I am ... nearly dead with work – and grief for the loss of my child."

By the end of 1840, Charles Dickens was as famous in the USA as he was in Britain. As soon the latest edition of one of his stories appeared in print, copies would be hastened onto a ship bound for New York. An often-quoted story tells that when the chapter in which Little Nell's fate was decided was due to arrive, New York's harbour was thronged with anxious readers. As the ship entered the port those on the ground were reported to have called up to those on board, "Is Little Nell alive?" and, when they heard that she had died, to have wept.

ABOVE The author's son, Alfred Tennyson Dickens, leaving the Old Curiosity Shop during his trip home from Australia in 1911.

RIGHT George Cattermole's illustration of the first chapter of *The Old Curiosity Shop*. It shows the narrator seeing Little Nell safely home, where her anxious grandfather has been waiting for her.

12

BARNABY RUDGE

Published in 1841, Barnaby Rudge *was Dickens's first historical novel. It is set in the eighteenth century and begins on a night in 1775 – interestingly, this is the same year in which Dickens's only other historical novel,* A Tale of Two Cities, *also begins.* Barnaby Rudge *opens with the story of a murder that had been committed 22 years before.*

The main focus of the story then shifts to five years later and centres on the Gordon Riots in London, a furious outpouring of anti-Catholic sentiment or "no popery". Dickens used factual sources to research the riots, which had taken place in 1780 and were associated with the agitator and MP Lord George Gordon.

The idea for *Barnaby Rudge* first came to Dickens in 1836, as the germ of a novel he entitled *Gabriel Varden*. He discussed it with the publisher John Macrone before changing his mind and deciding to write it as a serial for *Bentley's Miscellany*. *Barnaby Rudge* took a long time to come to fruition. Dickens completed both *Oliver Twist* and *Nicholas Nickleby* and kept the publisher Richard Bentley waiting for the promised chapters of his new book; he became very angry when Bentley advertised the "upcoming" serial in the magazine when Dickens had written only a couple of chapters. This led to an exchange of angry letters; Dickens began negotiating a new contract with the publishers Chapman & Hall and the book was transferred to their list. Although the novel's name had been changed, Gabriel remained one

of its central characters, but it is interesting to consider how, as Dickens started to write and the story developed, the character of Barnaby began to assume a far greater importance to the author than his original protagonist.

The two men could not be more different. Gabriel is "a round, red-faced, sturdy yeoman, with … a voice husky with good living, good sleeping, good humour and good health … Bluff, hale, hearty and in a green old age." Barnaby, by contrast, is the mentally deficient son of the supposedly murdered man. He eventually becomes involved with the rioters, and is classified by most as the "village idiot":

He was about three-and-twenty years old … His hair, of which he had a great profusion, was red, and hanging in disorder about his face and shoulders, gave to his restless looks an expression quite unearthly – enhanced by the paleness of his complexion, and the glassy lustre of his large

OPPOSITE An illustration of the Gordon Riots, which took place on 7 June 1780. A mob attacked Newgate Prison and set free the prisoners.

protruding eyes ... His dress was of green, clumsily trimmed here and there – apparently by his own hands – with gaudy lace ... The fluttered and confused disposition of all the motley scraps that formed his dress, bespoke ... the disorder of his mind.

Barnaby's constant companion as his story takes its course is his pet raven, Grip, an immortalizing of Dickens's own pet bird. The real Grip was a tyrannical pet who terrified the family's dogs into letting him eat all the best morsels from their bowls. Dickens adored the intelligent bird, who could talk and play tricks; after Grip died, he took his body to a taxidermist and then kept the stuffed bird in his study. Following the author's death, Grip was sold at auction, and today he can be seen in the Free Library of Philadelphia, USA.

Barnaby Rudge first appeared in weekly instalments in Dickens's magazine *Master Humphrey's Clock* (published by Chapman & Hall), and suddenly the block he seemed to have suffered from in the early stages of his planning dissipated. Needing to produce a new chapter every week was a challenging task, but Dickens became so engrossed in the story that he was soon far ahead of the publishing schedule.

While writing *Barnaby Rudge*, he began to explore the rights and wrongs of capital punishment. It was common practice at the time for people to attend public hangings of condemned prisoners (usually murderers) at London's Newgate Prison, and Dickens, wanting to write with feeling about public executions in his novel, went to see the execution of François Courvoisier, a Swiss valet who had murdered his aristocratic employer. The unsettling and chilling experience haunted him for many years and led him to write campaigning letters to newspapers. As is the case with *A Tale of Two Cities*, *Barnaby Rudge* is darker and contains less humour than the majority of Dickens's novels.

The Death of Grip

On 12 March 1841, Dickens wrote to his friend Daniel Maclise:

[Grip] expired to-day at a few minutes after twelve o'clock, at noon. He had been ailing for a few days ... I sent an express for the medical gentleman ... Under the influence of this medicine he recovered so far as to be able ... to bite Topping [the coachman]. His night was peaceful ... Toward eleven o'clock he was so much worse that it was found necessary to muffle the stable knocker. At half-past, or thereabouts, he was heard talking to himself about the horse and Topping's family.

He added that his children seemed "rather glad" the raven was dead, as he used to bite their ankles "but that was only in play".

ABOVE An image of Barnaby Rudge and his raven Grip from a later edition of Dickens's novel, drawn by FG Lewin.

LEFT Libberton's Wynd, Edinburgh, in the 1840s. In 1841, the year in which *Barnaby Rudge* was published, Dickens was awarded the Freedom of the City of Edinburgh.

OPPOSITE A self-portrait of Hablot Knight Browne (1815–82), aka "Phiz", the illustrator of *Barnaby Rudge*.

13

DICKENS &
NORTH AMERICA

*Charles Dickens first set foot on North American soil in 1842, when he was
29 years old. Charles, Catherine and her maid Anne Brown set sail from
Liverpool on the SS* Britannia, *and had "a most miserable voyage".*

On 20 January, the ship docked at Halifax in northeast Canada, where the author was received warmly and the town made "a most pleasant impression". Two days later, they reached Boston and were greeted by Dickens's temporary secretary, George Washington Putnam, who eased their journey through cultural and practical difficulties.

The party travelled extensively in the USA and Canada. Dickens gave speeches and he and Catherine attended banquets, took part in theatricals and received warm hospitality. Catherine's main task was to entertain unexpected visitors, who called constantly at their hotels when the author was trying to work. Throughout his travels, Dickens raised awareness of a subject close to his heart, a call for laws to be passed on international copyright; he carried with him a letter signed by 12 eminent British authors, including Alfred, Lord Tennyson.

He also visited prisons to inspect their conditions and travelled to Virginia to see the truth about slavery. The experience was soul-destroying, as he would later relate in

American Notes, published on his return: "In the negro car belonging to the train … were a mother and her children who had just been purchased; the husband and father being left behind with their old owner. The children cried the whole way, and the mother was misery's picture." Dickens was already a supporter of the Anti-Slavery League, and this experience made his beliefs even stronger. Unable to stomach the intended idea of travelling farther south, the party changed their itinerary.

The author wrote eagerly in letters about his plans to meet a community of Native Americans. In this he was to be frustrated, but by chance he met Pitchlynn, chief of the Choctaw tribe, on board a steamboat to St Louis. Dickens was disappointed to see the chief wearing "ordinary everyday" clothes. "[Pitchlynn] answered … that his race were losing many things besides their dress, and would soon be seen upon the earth no more: but he wore it at home, he added proudly."

From the very beginning, Americans loved Dickens. Even in 1842, he received the kind of adulation that would later be reserved for pop stars; he wrote to

ABOVE The Cunard Line's first transatlantic liner, *Britannia*, seen here leaving Boston in 1847. Charles and Catherine Dickens sailed to America on *Britannia* in 1842. They were both very seasick.

Family Portrait by Maclise

When Charles and Catherine Dickens departed from London on 2 January 1842, they left behind their four children, Charley, Mamie, Katey and Walter (who was less than a year old). Their artist friend Daniel Maclise (1806–70) presented Catherine with a beautiful sketch of the children, together with the family's pet raven, Grip, so she could carry them with her at all times during her travels. The house at Devonshire Terrace was let to tenants in the family's absence, and the children moved into a smaller house in nearby Osnaburgh Street, where they were looked after by servants under the care of Uncle Fred.

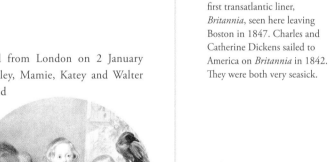

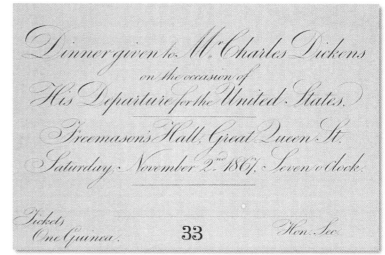

John Forster: "I can do nothing that I want to do, go nowhere where I want to go, and see nothing that I want to see. If I turn into the street, I am followed by a multitude."

He also made a number of true friends, including the poet Henry Wadsworth Longfellow, who would later come to England several times, staying with the family and impressing the young Dickens children. In contrast, Edgar Allan Poe, who met Dickens in Philadelphia in 1842, later ended their friendship over a literary dispute. Poe disapproved of an article he erroneously believed was written by Dickens.

After almost six months of travelling, Charles and Catherine set sail for England on the *George Washington*. They arrived in Liverpool on 29 June and hurried to London and their children – eluding journalists by arriving home

earlier than they were expected. The children were thrilled to have their parents back, and Charles and Catherine never wanted to go on such a journey again without them.

Although Dickens was impressed with many aspects of North American life, by the end of his tour he was writing dispirited letters home. His new book, *American Notes*, proved a bitter disappointment to many of the Americans he had met, and several promising friendships, such as that with Washington Irving, did not survive its publication. His two most ferocious criticisms were about slavery and the American press. *American Notes* and *Martin Chuzzlewit* would sully Dickens's reputation in the USA for many years to come.

It took 25 years for Charles Dickens to return to the USA, on a tour in November 1867 that had been postponed for several years due to the American Civil

Mark Twain on Dickens

On Dickens's second visit, a prominent member of his audience was not impressed. The newly famous Mark Twain's report on Dickens's readings in New York City seethes with irritation (and envy). Twain complained about his fellow author's pronunciation skills, his English accent, his choice of clothes, the way he walked and that Dickens wasn't handsome enough, commenting: "Somehow this puissant god seemed to be only a man, after all. How the great do tumble from their high pedestals when we see them in common human flesh."

RIGHT During his American tour of 1867–68, Charles Dickens was photographed by the prestigious photographer Jeremiah Gurney (1812–86), at his studio in New York City.

OPPOSITE LEFT Charles and Catherine Dickens met the poet Henry Wadsworth Longfellow in 1842, during their trip to North America. He later visited them in England, where the Dickens children were fascinated by him.

OPPOSITE RIGHT This invitation, priced at one guinea, allowed the owner to attend a farewell dinner for Charles Dickens before the author left for his second trip to America in 1867.

"AU REVOIR!"

War. The USA welcomed a very different Dickens from the exuberant young man of the 1840s, complete with a pretty young wife. At 55, he returned grizzled, much aged, in pain and on his own. He had longed to bring Ellen Ternan with him, but had finally been persuaded by his friends and agent that the USA retained its puritanical roots and travelling with his young actress mistress would be the worst possible PR move. His overall health was poor and for the past few years, he had suffered almost constant pain in his left foot.

As he had done in 1842, he began his reading tour in Boston, where he met his American publisher, James T Fields. James and his wife Annie became close friends with the author, whom they both idolized, and Annie would become one of Dickens's most regular correspondents. After almost two weeks recuperating from the sea voyage – and growing restless – at Boston's Parker House hotel, Dickens began a gruelling schedule, completing over 400 speaking engagements in six months. After the costs of the tour and currency conversion had been deducted, he had earned over £19,000 for six months' work. Despite its financial rewards and the warm friendships that he made, he often found the experience debilitating and lonely. He missed Ellen and his family, and the still-persistent memory of the Staplehurst rail crash made the long train journeys psychologically challenging.

While the overall mood was one of adulation, not all Americans were welcoming: for some, the wounds of *American Notes* and *Martin Chuzzlewit* still smarted. In common with Mark Twain, the *New York Herald* was determined to be the one newspaper whose coverage of Dickens's tour was inflammatory and unflattering. Overall, however, the tour was a great success and cemented the author's reputation in the USA permanently.

A lavish farewell dinner was held in New York on 18 April 1868, although the usually fastidiously punctual Dickens arrived almost an hour late, his foot having proved so troublesome that he had been unable to finish dressing. Two days later, he struggled through his final reading, then collapsed into bed. He left the USA on 22 April amid great excitement – helping his tour manager George Dolby to make a dramatic escape from the New York Collector of Taxes, who wanted to arrest Dolby for not declaring Dickens's earnings (despite an indemnity that had already been granted to them). After a few days on board the *Russia*, Dickens's health seemed to improve. The ship docked in Liverpool on 1 May.

THE BRITISH LION IN AMERICA (Charles Dickens).

BELOW This caricature of Dickens, captioned "The British Lion in America", was published in the *Daily Joker* in New York. It is based on the famous photograph taken by Jeremiah Gurney.

OPPOSITE In this illustration – *Au Revoir!* – from 1867, Charles Dickens is bid farewell by a number of his literary characters.

14

MARTIN CHUZZLEWIT

The complicated plot of Martin Chuzzlewit *is built up around the idea of greed. At the start of the novel, old Martin Chuzzlewit, a wealthy eccentric, falls ill while travelling through Salisbury and takes up residence at the local inn, the Blue Boar. The inn is not far from the home of an architect, Mr Pecksniff, and his daughters Charity and Mercy.*

Mr Pecksniff is awaiting the arrival of his new apprentice, Martin Chuzzlewit, the grandson of the man now residing at the Blue Boar. In a very short while, Dickens has set the stage for the action to follow: the hypocrisy of Pecksniff – whose eventual comeuppance is a joy to the reader – as well as the perceived futures of his daughters and the machinations of the extended Chuzzlewit family.

In *Martin Chuzzlewit*, Dickens created such unforgettable characters as young Martin's loyal and unswervingly optimistic friend Mark Tapley; the swindler Montague Tigg; the private detective Nadgett; and the idealized sibling relationship between Ruth and Tom Pinch. Most famous of all is Mrs Sairey Gamp, a drunk nurse and midwife, whom Dickens used not only to provide a ghoulish humour but to expose the problems of the Victorian public medical service and its lack of regulations.

Martin Chuzzlewit saw Dickens begin to write in a new way. With his previous novels he had done little forward planning, but *Martin Chuzzlewit*, published in 1843–44, was plotted in advance. Although Dickens was pleased with the way the book was progressing, his readers felt differently. The first monthly episodes of the novel sold far fewer copies than those of his previous books. For the first time since he had become famous, Dickens's popularity began to wane. Searching for a solution, something that would grab the public's imagination, Dickens hit upon the idea of sending Martin to the USA, allowing the novelist to give free rein to the wonderful fictional ideas and characters that had presented themselves to him while he was on his travels.

The portrayal of the USA in *Martin Chuzzlewit* was not favourable. Martin journeys to the ironically named Eden. It is not a paradise. Dickens based Eden on Cairo in Illinois, a slur the people of Illinois were very slow to forgive. The cause of even more fury was Dickens's

OPPOSITE Dickens described the hypocritical Mr Pecksniff with the words: "Perhaps there never was a more moral man ... especially in his conversation and correspondence."

portrayal of the much-loved Mississippi: "great father of rivers, who (praise be to Heaven) has no young children like him! An enormous ditch, sometimes two or three miles wide, running liquid mud, six miles an hour.... For two days we toiled up this foul stream." Dickens's acerbic wit was exacerbated by the unflattering letters he had been receiving continually from the USA ever since he had published *American Notes*.

He was not notably more flattering about Britain. On first envisioning *Martin Chuzzlewit*, he had decided to set the opening scenes in Cornwall. In October 1842, Dickens and his friends John Forster, Clarkson Stanfield (1793–1867) and Daniel Maclise set off by train to visit Dickens's parents in Devon, en route to Cornwall. Dickens had written to a friend that he desired to see "the very dreariest and most desolate" part of the Cornish coast. They travelled around Cornwall in a private carriage, visiting tin mines, churches, beaches, cliffs, the castle at Tintagel and Land's End. When he began writing, Dickens changed his mind about using Cornwall as his location; instead, the countryside in the novel is that around Salisbury in Wiltshire.

Unusually, the eponymous hero, young Martin, is not as heroic at the start of *Martin Chuzzlewit* as readers might expect. He is a flawed, selfish and at times uncaring man, whose journey throughout the book is one of self-discovery and self-improvement. His grandfather also has an epiphany and learns to be less proud. By the end of the novel, both Martin Chuzzlewits, old and young, have become much happier.

Although the initial sales of the novel proved disappointing, it eventually began to sell well. This was helped in no small amount by the novella Dickens had written at the same time, *A Christmas Carol*.

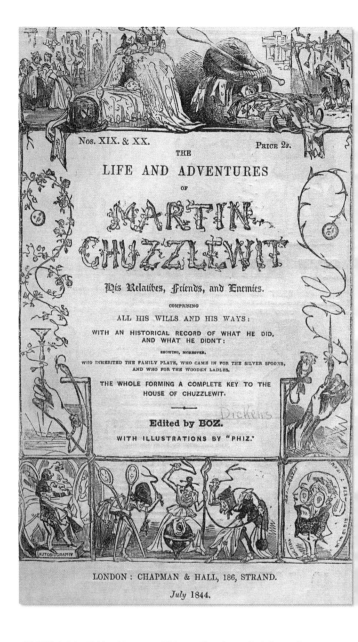

ABOVE A July 1844 publication of *Martin Chuzzlewit* which featured Dickens's first real detective, Mr Nadgett.

OPPOSITE TOP A wood engraving from a nineteenth century American edition of *Martin Chuzzlewit*. It shows Mr Moddle attempting to kiss Miss Pecksniff's hand, but missing it.

OPPOSITE BOTTOM Dickens wrote part of *Martin Chuzzlewit* while on holiday at Cobley's Farm in Finchley, north London, in March 1843.

HE KISSED MISS PECKSNIFF'S SNUFFERS IN THE PASSAGE . . . . MEANING TO HAVE KISSED HER HAND, BUT MISSING IT.

15

A CHRISTMAS CAROL

In October 1843, Charles Dickens paid a visit to Manchester.
He had been invited to give a talk at the First Annual Soirée of the
Athenaeum, a charity that aimed to bring education to working men and
women. His adored sister Fanny was living in Manchester, so he took the
opportunity to visit her.

Fanny was a gifted musician and singer, as was her husband, Henry Burnett. Yet she was also a sickly woman, a consumptive who would die much too young. Of the Burnetts' two sons, one was robust and healthy, the other disabled and often unwell. Dickens felt particularly keenly for this little nephew, who would inspire Paul Dombey in *Dombey and Son* and Tiny Tim in *A Christmas Carol*.

The idea for a story that emphasized the plight of poor children had been brewing for some time. At the start of 1843, Dickens had been appalled to read a government report on the lives of children who worked in mines and factories. Prior to his visit to Manchester, he had visited a "ragged school" (a charity school that provided the poorest children with free education, plus often food and accommodation), where his eyes were opened to the abject poverty on the streets of London. Many of the pupils were already embroiled in lives of crime, including prostitution. The thing that struck him most was their deeply entrenched ignorance and how dangerous that ignorance made them. He wrote in the weekly paper *The*

Examiner, "Side by side with Crime, Disease and Misery in England, Ignorance is always brooding, and is always certain to be found."

In Manchester, he witnessed an even greater depth of poverty and misery. He realized the problem was even worse than in London, the poor people of Manchester having been struck repeatedly by the advances of the Industrial Revolution. As machines took over the work once performed by people and increasing numbers of desperate workers migrated from Ireland, whole families could be seen starving on the streets of Manchester.

On returning to London, Dickens acted on his promise to strike "a hammer blow" in favour of "the Poor Man's child". It took him just six weeks to write *A Christmas Carol*, the story of Ebenezer Scrooge, a hard-hearted old miser whose life and personality are changed by the three spirits of Christmas he encounters one Christmas Eve. The characters of Ebenezer Scrooge, Jacob Marley, Bob Cratchit and Tiny Tim are known throughout the world, aided by countless film and television adaptations. Yet how many people remember

ABOVE One of John Leech's illustrations from *A Christmas Carol* depicting the ghost of Jacob Marley appearing to his former business partner Ebenezer Scrooge.

RIGHT This edition of *A Christmas Carol* belonged to Charles Dickens's father, John Dickens.

the two children, Ignorance and Want, whose scrawny, starved limbs are seen poking from beneath the robes of the Ghost of Christmas Present? To Dickens, they were two of the most important characters in the novella, but sadly most adaptations pay scant – if any – attention to these pivotal figures.

The first print run for *A Christmas Carol*, in December 1843, was 6,000. This sold out in five days. The novella was aimed at making readers realize that they themselves were directly responsible for the poor people they passed on the streets every day. The book also helped Dickens financially: with the publication of *Oliver Twist* (1838), *Nicholas Nickleby* (1839) and *The Old Curiosity Shop* (1841), he had already gained international fame; with *A Christmas Carol*, he gained international adulation. When *A Christmas Carol* was declared "a national institution" by a critic, the novelist William Makepeace Thackeray responded that it was actually a "national benefit".

In 1867, Dickens spent Christmas in the USA and on Christmas Eve, he read *A Christmas Carol* to an

audience in Boston. In the audience was a Mr Fairbanks, a factory owner from Chicago. According to legend, Mr Fairbanks was so moved by Dickens's reading that he had a Scrooge-like conversion and vowed to become a better employer and a more charitable man. He declared he would close the factory every 25 December, giving all his workers the day off. He also gave Christmas turkeys to all his employees.

Dickens's Christmas Books

Although most people only know *A Christmas Carol*, Dickens actually wrote four more Christmas books: *The Chimes* (1844), *The Cricket on the Hearth* (1845), *The Battle of Life* (1846) and *The Haunted Man* (1848). In later years, he concentrated on writing seasonal Christmas stories for his weekly magazines, *Household Words* (1850–58) and *All the Year Round* (1859–67).

RIGHT Trotty Veck from *The Chimes*, illustrated by Joseph Clayton Clarke. Dickens wrote *The Chimes* while living in Genoa; he described his new Christmas story as "a plea for the poor".

16

SOCIAL CONSCIENCE

A prime force behind much of Dickens's work was his social conscience, which led him to draw public attention to hardship and injustices of the time. This had its roots in his childhood, beginning when his family was sent to debtors' prison.

During the months of working in the blacking factory, the young Dickens walked the streets of London every day: from his lodging house to work, to the prison to eat supper with his family, and then on the lonely, frightening, dark walk back home. He became accustomed to seeing terrible scenes, witnessing the depths to which impoverished people had to sink. He saw starvation, alcoholism, violence, deprivation and misery. He would never forget this time.

As an adult, Dickens never talked about his father's disgrace or his own time as a child labourer. The only people who knew the truth about his childhood were his wife Catherine and his best friend, John Forster. Although Dickens was determined to keep his own past secret, he was equally determined to use his talent to tell his readers about the social injustices he knew existed on the streets of London. In *Oliver Twist* he revealed the truth about England's workhouses. He returned to the theme in several of his articles, including "Pet Prisoners" (*Household Words* 27 April 1850), in which he compares the treatment of and diet given to inmates of a prison with those of the residents of a workhouse; the criminals are given notably better treatment and more food. Similarly, in "A Nightly Scene in London" (*Household Words*, 26 January 1856) he describes the women he saw on the streets of Whitechapel, one of the most deprived areas of East London. Five homeless women were huddled outside the workhouse, which was already full. They had nowhere to sleep and nothing to eat. Dickens describes them as "... five bundles of rags. They were motionless and had no resemblance to the human form."

Dickens was not in favour of all charitable causes – and was certainly not in favour of all charitable figures. The hypocrisy of many charities was something he found frustrating, and he lampooned this hypocrisy in his writing, notably in *Bleak House.* Mrs Jellyby and Mrs Pardiggle are far more concerned with saving "heathens" overseas than with confronting the problems directly in front of them, such as Mrs Jellyby's own neglected children and Jo the ragged crossing sweeper, a desperately poor labouring child with no family and no means of eating except the meagre handouts he gets from

ABOVE Dickens campaigned
fervently for children's rights.
He wrote articles about the
appalling conditions of child
labourers, created heart-
rending child characters and
supported children's charities.

RIGHT The forbidding façade
of Clerkenwell Workhouse.
In *Oliver Twist*, Dickens
wrote passionately about the
iniquities of the workhouse
system and the careless cruelty
of the people in charge.

OPPOSITE Brook Street
Ragged and Industrial School.
In 1852, Dickens visited
such a school and was deeply
affected: he found the squalid
surroundings "miserable" but
was impressed by teachers and
pupils.

LEFT Urania Cottage was
in Shepherd's Bush, then a
pretty little suburb west of
London. Dickens organized
the household utilities and
supplies, and dealt with day-to-
day problems.

Angela Burdett-Coutts

One of the wealthiest women in the British Empire, Angela Burdett-Coutts
(1814–1906) acquired her fortune by a twist of fate. Her grandfather was
Thomas Coutts (1735–1822), one of the founders of Britain's most prestigious
and wealthy bank. Unexpectedly, he chose to leave his vast fortune to his
granddaughter. Angela was deeply concerned about the deprivations she saw in
London, especially the prostitutes who worked near her home every night, many
of whom were children, and about the homeless, especially the vast number of
elderly people who were left to starve on the streets. So she chose to use her
funds to help the city's poor, abused and overlooked.

Angela met Dickens in the 1830s and they created a number of charitable
schemes. Their friendship survived for two decades; more than 600 letters between
them survive today. In 1858, Angela became furious with Dickens when he began
an affair with a young actress and separated from his wife. Angela sided with
Catherine Dickens and their joint philanthropic projects came to an end.

sweeping the streets. *Oliver Twist* and *Bleak House* also saw Dickens deal with the taboo subject of illegitimacy; he highlights the issue of how unfair it was of society to treat illegitimate children as though they themselves had committed a crime.

Children were always a subject very close to Dickens's heart. His youngest daughter, Dora, died when she was eight months old. In 1852, the year after Dora's death, a new hospital opened in London. The Hospital for Sick Children on Great Ormond Street was much needed and much in need of funds. Dickens was one of the first contributors to the hospital's fundraising efforts; he also helped to publicize it by writing an emotive article in *Household Words*. In *Nicholas Nickleby* he exposed the existence of Yorkshire schools, institutions in the north of England where unwanted children – illegitimate children, stepchildren, disabled children – were sent and where they were neglected and beaten. Within two years

of the novel's publication, almost every Yorkshire school had been closed down.

In several of his novels, including *Oliver Twist, David Copperfield* and *The Old Curiosity Shop*, Dickens highlighted the evils of prostitution and domestic violence. Together with Angela Burdett-Coutts he set up an unusual new project, a "Home for Homeless Women" in west London. Urania Cottage was in the new suburb of Shepherd's Bush, five kilometres (three miles) from the centre of town. Possible residents were suggested to Dickens by charity workers and wardens of women's prisons. At Urania Cottage, the women were taught basic domestic skills. When their education was complete, they were expected to travel to Canada or Australia, where they would be able to find work as a domestic servant or to marry a working man in need of a wife. The project was not as successful as Dickens and Burdett-Coutts had hoped, but it was nonetheless an innovative scheme ahead of its time.

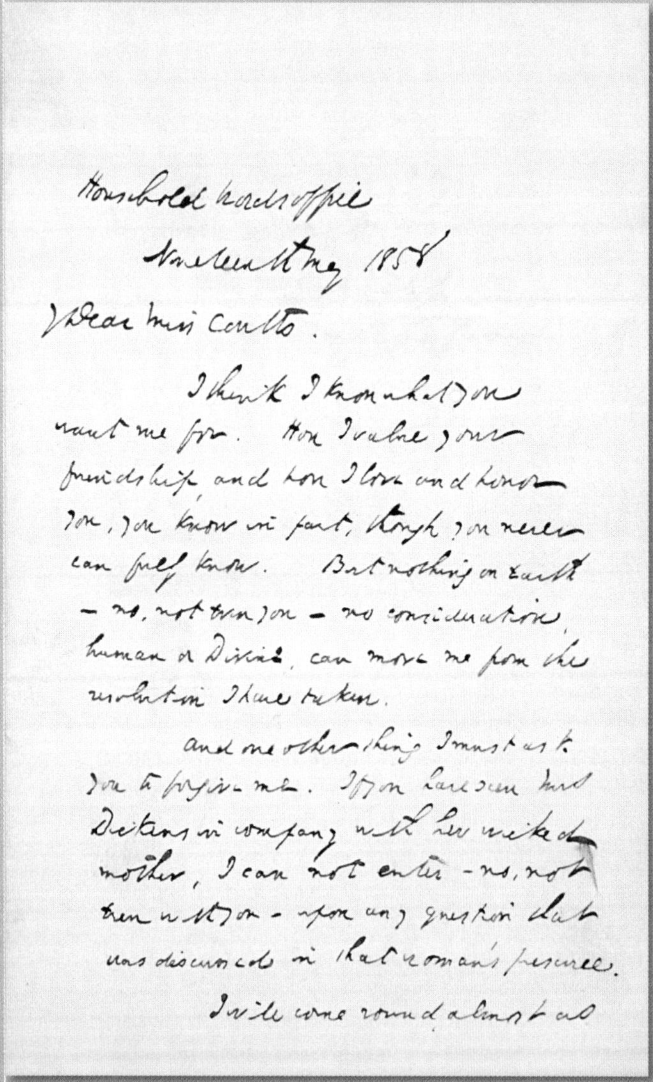

Household Words office
Nineteenth May 1858
My Dear Miss Coutts.

I think I know what you
want me for. How I value your
friendship, and how I love and honor
you, you know in part, though you never
can fully know. But nothing on earth
— no, not even you — no consideration,
human or Divine, can move me from the
resolution I have taken.

And one other thing I must ask
you to forgive me. If you have seen Mrs
Dickens in company with her wicked
mother, I can not enter — no, not
even with you — upon any question that
was discussed in that woman's presence.

I will come round almost as

soon as your messenger; but I foresee that
there is nothing left to us to say.

My Dear Miss Coutts

Ever affectionately
and faithfully yours
CD.

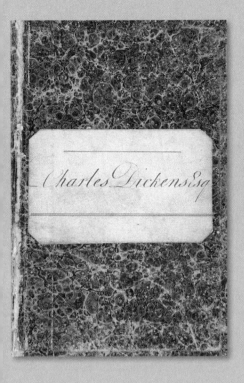

RIGHT Charles Dickens opened his account at Coutts Bank after becoming friends with Angela Burdett-Coutts, the unexpected heir of the banker Thomas Coutts (her grandfather). This account book details the minutiae of Dickens's daily financial transactions.

THE ITALIAN YEAR

In 1844, the Dickens family embarked on an adventure. Charles was growing restless. He had been working solidly and prolifically, completing Martin Chuzzlewit *and* A Christmas Carol; *he was exhausted and bored with routine. What he needed was excitement and inspiration.*

Catherine was also worn out, after giving birth to her fifth child, Frank, in the middle of a grey and cold English winter. The solution was to pack up and leave England, albeit temporarily.

Dickens ordered a special travelling carriage, big enough to accommodate 11 people: himself, Catherine, Georgina, the five children and three servants – as well as the dog, Timber. On 2 July, the "English travelling-carriage of considerable proportions" began a two-week journey from London, through France and Switzerland, to the village of Albaro, outside Genoa in Italy. Dickens relates the journey with humour in the travelogue he wrote about their months abroad, *Pictures from Italy* (1846).

Dickens had long been seduced by the idea of living in Italy. He had decided to base himself near Genoa because it was in Albaro that the Romantic poet Lord Byron had composed part of his epic, *Don Juan*. One of Dickens's friends, Angus Fletcher, a Scottish sculptor,

was also living near Genoa and it was he who arranged the family's accommodation. Dickens wanted to live in the house in which Byron had stayed, but it was in a bad condition and not at all suitable for a family with young children, so Fletcher found them an idyllic pink-coloured house, Villa di Bella Vista, known to all the locals as Villa di Bagnarello. It had superb views of the sea, but Dickens did not like it and did not deem it worthy of its high rent. He called it the "pink gaol" and complained that its owner, a Signor Bagnarello, was merely a "drunken butcher". But despite the author's many grumblings, he was not unhappy at the villa and adored its location; as he wrote to John Forster, "When

LEFT George Gordon, sixth Lord Byron (1788–1824), was Dickens's inspiration for visiting Genoa. He wanted to write in the same place in which the poet had worked on *Don Juan*.

the sun sets clearly, by Heaven, it is majestic."

His happiness was complete when, in September, the family moved into a much more illustrious home – a wing of the splendid Palazzo Peschiere whose walls were adorned with frescoes dating back three centuries. "There is not in Italy ... a lovelier residence than Palazzo Peschiere, or Palace of the Fishponds ... It is more like an enchanted place in an Eastern story than a grave and sober lodging." The children and Timber played happily for hours in the huge gardens filled with statues, fountains and shady trees. Timber was so plagued by Italian fleas – which Dickens was convinced were far more tenacious than those in England – that it was decided to shave all the dog's fur off for the duration of their stay.

Although the Dickens children spent all of their Italian adventure near Genoa, Charles, Catherine and sometimes Georgina took journeys around the country. In Rome, Dickens experienced frightening imaginings of what life must have been like under the brutality of the ancient Romans. He wrote in a heartfelt manner of visiting the Coliseum where he envisioned terrible scenes "no language can describe". In *Pictures from Italy* he commented, "Never in its bloodiest prime, can the sight of the gigantic Coliseum, full and running over with the lustiest life, have moved one heart as it must move all who look upon it now,

a ruin. GOD be thanked: a ruin!" A visit to the Vatican impressed the author in a far less sombre fashion. He found the pomp and ceremony ridiculous and compared the sight of the Pope being carried by his guards to that of a children's effigy of Guy Fawkes about to be placed on a bonfire: "A bundle of matches and a lantern, would have made it perfect".

In the mid-nineteenth century, Italy was a popular location for impoverished British people, as the cost of living meant they could enjoy a far superior lifestyle to anything they could afford at home. Although Dickens was earning well, living in a palace would never have been possible in London. He revelled in this new style of living, such a world away from the childhood that continued to haunt him. In Italy he was renowned and recognized, but not uncomfortably famous; he could walk for miles in warm sunshine and never feel cold rain; he adored the climate, the views, the people he met, the musical language he heard all around him. He made a slow start in learning Italian until he was shamed by their English cook, who picked up the language far more quickly than he did; this spurred him on to speak it more fluently. Dickens later said that he would have been content to live in Italy permanently, but Catherine missed England and wanted to return home. They left for London in the spring of 1845.

18

DOMBEY AND SON

Dealings with the Firm of Dombey and Son: Wholesale, Retail and for Exportation, to give the novel its original name, was begun while the Dickens family were living in Switzerland for a few months. In early 1846, Dickens had again become restless. At the end of the previous year, he had started a new venture, helping to set up the Daily News *and becoming its editor.*

He began publishing *Pictures from Italy* in serial form in the newspaper. He commissioned many friends and family members to work for the new publication, including his father and his father-in-law. The *Daily News* encountered a number of frustrating teething problems, and within a few weeks, Dickens chose to pass on the role of editor to John Forster. The newspaper had hampered his writing routine and he was finding it impossible to get started on his proposed new novel.

Missing the excitement of living in Italy and frustrated with the routine of his London life, he rented the Villa Rosemont in Lausanne, Switzerland. Here he had "a little Study, not unlike a large plate-warmer" in which to write, yet despite his exciting new surroundings, he remained in a restless frame of mind for some time after the family's arrival in Switzerland. Just days before beginning his new novel (an event he celebrated in capital letters – "BEGAN DOMBEY!" – in a letter to Forster), he wrote of his uncertainty about the coming weeks: "My movements depend so much on my industry here, and my industry depends so much on the humour I am in from day to day." This feeling of frustration and a melancholy atmosphere pervades *Dombey and Son*, whose final episode was published in April 1848.

One of the prominent themes of the novel is the inequality between male and female children: Paul Dombey is a sickly child, yet his father channels all his love and plans for the future into him, ignoring his healthy and able daughter, Florence, purely because she is a girl. Dickens took great pains to ensure that Mr

ABOVE Phiz's illustration from *Dombey and Son* shows little Paul Dombey with the severe Mrs Pipchin, who runs a children's boarding house in Brighton where Paul is sent for his health.

Dombey's treatment of his daughter would be reflected in Paul's treatment of him: as Paul lies ill and dying, it is not to his father that he turns, but to Florence, whom he adores. In July 1846, Dickens sent John Forster the first four chapters as well as an outline of the rest of the novel; the accompanying letter shows he intended to sacrifice little Paul from the outset, to encourage the public to think about the cruelty of sexual inequality.

Dickens often drew his characters from life. In *Dombey and Son*, little Paul was inspired by Dickens's nephew Harry Burnett, the son of his sister Fanny. A sickly child who suffered from an undiagnosed disability, he was fated to die in 1849, just a few months after his mother. As well as being the inspiration for Paul Dombey, Harry had previously inspired the character of Tiny Tim in *A Christmas Carol*. After reading the chapter about the death of Paul Dombey, the actor William Charles Macready rushed to visit Dickens but admitted he was unable to talk to his friend because he could not stop crying. The whole country seemed to have been affected by the death of little Paul – Dickens had moved an entire nation to tears. Before writing the scene the author had wandered the streets in despair, agonizing over his decision to kill Paul, just as he was said to have been "inconsolable" over the death of Little Nell in *The Old Curiosity Shop*.

Less affecting but equally drawn from life, Mrs Pipchin immortalized the landlady with whom the young Charles had lived while his parents were in prison. The proprietress of a children's boarding house, she is described as: "a marvellous ill-favoured, ill-conditioned old lady, of a stooping figure, with a mottled face, like bad marble, a hook nose, and a hard grey eye ... She was generally spoken of as a 'great manager' of children; and the secret of her management was to give them everything that they didn't like and nothing that they did."

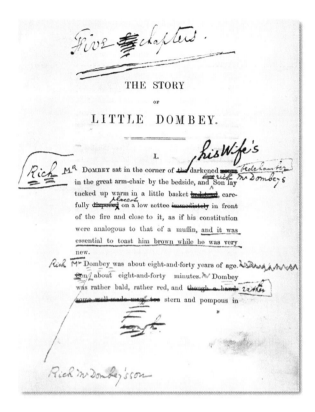

ABOVE A proof copy of the first page of *Dombey and Son*, with Charles Dickens's corrections written by hand.

RIGHT This colour engraving is by Phiz, the illustrator of *Dombey and Son*. It depicts Mr Dombey with James Carker, the man who elopes with Mr Dombey's second wife.

19

DICKENS
AND RELIGION

Inasmuch as Dickens showed an interest in religion, it was in terms of moral stance rather than theological belief. His parents, John and Elizabeth Dickens, baptized their children into the Church of England.

But religion does not seem to have played much part in their family life. Charles's older sister, Fanny, would later tell her church minister that she was brought up "without any serious ideas of religion".

Throughout Dickens's writing runs a theme of anger at religious hypocrisy. Characters including Mrs Jellyby in *Bleak House* and Mr Pecksniff in *Martin Chuzzlewit* are ridiculed as churchgoers who call themselves Christians yet make no effort to help those in need around them. In the early 1840s, after his first visit to the USA, Dickens turned from his token acceptance of Anglicanism and became a Unitarian. He wrote to a friend that he had joined the Unitarians because he was "disgusted with our Established Church, and its Puseyisms, and daily outrages on common sense and humanity", and because he believed the Unitarians "would do something for human improvement if they could; and practise charity and toleration". Dickens was particularly impressed by the stance the Unitarians took against slavery, a practice that was still happening in many parts of the world.

The author attended his first Unitarian services at the Essex Street chapel in London, before discovering a

ABOVE Rochester Cathedral in Kent, where Charles Dickens requested to be buried. Queen Victoria, however, insisted he be buried in London's Westminster Abbey.

OPPOSITE Dickens's portrayal of Fagin led to accusations of anti-Semitism. As an apology to the Jewish community, he later created Mr Riah in *Our Mutual Friend*.

chapel closer to his home, in Little Portland Street near Regent's Park. For many years, he rented a pew in the chapel for himself and his family, for which he paid £7 a year. By the late 1840s, the family seem to have attended the chapel less and less frequently, and towards the end of his life, Dickens returned to Anglicanism. When he moved to Kent, he attended services at his local church and in his will, he requested that he be buried at the Anglican cathedral in Rochester, Kent. Queen Victoria overruled his will and decreed that Charles Dickens, as the country's most popular writer, should be interred at Poet's Corner in Westminster Abbey, London.

There has been some discussion as to whether Dickens was anti-Semitic. Because of the portrayal of Fagin in *Oliver Twist* – and the fact that, in the first edition of the novel, in 1838, Fagin's character was often referred to as "the Jew" – the accusation has often been levelled, despite the fact that of the many hundreds of villains Dickens created, only one was Jewish. However, nineteenth-century Britain was a xenophobic society in which almost anyone who was not white, upper class and of the Anglican faith was viewed with suspicion. Dickens was writing in the atmosphere of the time: the language used in *Oliver Twist* was contemporary and not intended to be offensive.

Several years after the book's publication, Dickens's friend Eliza Davis, who was Jewish, told him that many of her friends were angry with him for focusing on Fagin's religion, so Dickens went through the later editions of the book and changed the language so Fagin became "the old man" instead of "the Jew". In 1864, Dickens began working on *Our Mutual Friend*, in which the Jewish character Mr Riah, a truly good and honourable person, can be seen as his apology to the Jewish community for any offence caused by his creation of Fagin. Most modern-day adaptations of *Oliver Twist* concentrate more closely on Fagin's religion than Dickens did in the original novel.

The Life of Our Lord

In 1934, a previously unknown book by Charles Dickens was published – 64 years after the author's death. *The Life of Our Lord* had been written for the Dickens children and carefully guarded by Charles Dickens, who would not allow it even to leave the house for fear someone would make a copy and publish it. He begins the story with the words "My dear children" and talks directly to them throughout. In one passage, he explains about the strange-sounding animals mentioned in the Bible: "You never saw a locust, because they belong to that country near Jerusalem, which is a great way off. So do camels, but I think you have seen a camel? At all events they are brought over here, sometimes; and if you would like to see one, I will shew you one." The Dickens family stipulated that the book could not be seen by the general public until there were none of Charles and Catherine's children still living. Sir Henry Fielding Dickens died in 1933 and it was published the following year.

20

DICKENS'S EXTENDED FAMILY

It is often assumed that Dickens was extremely rich, yet in reality, the more money he made, the larger the number of needy dependents he seemed to gain.

In addition to his ever-grasping parents and the needs of his children (many of whom inherited the family tendency of getting into debt), he was responsible for several of his siblings and their spouses and children.

John & Elizabeth Dickens

After being released from the Marshalsea, thanks to a small inheritance left to John Dickens, the author's parents returned to living beyond their means. In 1834, John was arrested again; Charles Dickens paid his father's debts and invited his younger brother Fred to live with him at Furnival's Inn. Once Dickens began to make a name for himself, his father started giving his son's name to creditors.

A letter Dickens wrote to John Forster explains his frustration: "Directly I build up a hundred pounds one of my dear relations comes and knocks it down again." After he was truly financially secure, Dickens was able to find the situation more amusing. He wrote a comical letter to Georgina Hogarth in 1860, after his father's death and towards the end of his mother's life: "I found my mother yesterday, much better than I had supposed ... Helen and Letitia were poulticing her poor head, and, the instant she saw me, she plucked up a spirit and asked for 'a pound'!"

Fanny Burnett (1810–48)

Fanny, a talented singer and musician, was two years older than Charles, and he adored her. As a boarding pupil at the Royal Academy of Music, Fanny had avoided the misery of being imprisoned in the Marshalsea. In *A Christmas Carol*, the young Ebenezer Scrooge is reminded of his loving sister, Fanny, or "little Fan".

Dickens was devastated by Fanny's death from consumption at the age of 38. She had two sons, one of whom, Harry, was disabled and died soon after she did. Dickens paid several doctors in the vain hope they would save her life. After Fanny's death, Dickens gave financial help to her widower, Henry Burnett, and their remaining son, Charles.

Letitia Austin (1816–93)

In 1837, Dickens's younger sister, Letitia, married the architect and civil engineer Henry Austin. Dickens was friends with Austin, who understood his problems with his parents. Austin became General Secretary of the Board of Health, campaigning, among other things, for a change to sanitation laws.

When Austin died, in 1860, Dickens fought for Letitia's rights to a government pension. He also supported her financially. The two siblings remained close and Letitia mourned Dickens greatly when he died. She outlived all her siblings, dying in 1893 at the age of 75.

Fred Dickens (1820–68)

Charles gave Fred a home at the age of 14, paid for his education and helped him find work. Fred, however, was easily bored and changed jobs regularly. In 1848, he married 18-year-old Anna Weller: his eldest brother strongly disapproved, causing a rift that would never be healed.

The marriage was not happy, and in 1858 Fred and Anna obtained a legal separation, which caused a scandal. Unable to pay alimony, Fred ran away to France. When he he returned to England, he was arrested and sent to the Queen's Bench debtors' prison.

Fred died a 48-year-old alcoholic who had spent his last years alternately berating his brother for not helping him and trying to squeeze money out of him. After hearing of his brother's death, Dickens raged in a letter to John Forster about Fred's "wasted life".

Alfred Dickens (1822–60)

Alfred was still a baby when the family moved into the Marshalsea. He was the most responsible of all the novelist's siblings, and became an engineer with a promising future. In the 1840s, Alfred worked on the York, Malton and Scarborough Railway and was an engineer on the Malton and Driffield railway line.

He became deeply concerned with issues of sanitation, poor health and poverty and i n 1855, published an important engineering report, which directly influenced the government and local authorities to start changing sanitary conditions around the country. Charles Dickens was very proud of his brother's achievements.

Tragically, Alfred died of pleurisy at the age of 38, leaving his widow Helen and their five children in financial trouble. Charles immediately moved the family close to his own home in London and looked after them.

Augustus Dickens (1827–66)

The baby of the family, Augustus was born when Charles Dickens was 15. Charles found Augustus a job and a place to live as soon as he finished school, and Augustus initially seemed a credit to his brother. In 1848, Augustus married Harriett Lovell. Little is known about the marriage, except they had no children and Harriett was in poor health, suffering from a condition that caused her to go blind.

In the mid-1850s, Augustus left his job and attempted to set himself up in business. At around the same time, Fred introduced him to a colleague's sister, Bertha Phillips. Augustus and Bertha became lovers and, in late 1856, she became pregnant. The couple ran away to America, calling themselves Mr and Mrs Dickens. They had seven children, of whom only three survived. In London, the abandoned Harriett was cared for by her husband's siblings, Letitia and Charles, who had no further communication with Augustus or Bertha or ever saw their children.

LEFT This portrait by Samuel Laurence is of Fanny Burnett (née Dickens). The author adored his older sister and tried desperately – and in vain – to find a doctor who could cure her consumption.

21

DAVID COPPERFIELD

When Dickens started planning Great Expectations *in October 1860, he wrote to his friend John Forster, "I read* David Copperfield *again the other day, and was affected by it to a degree you would hardly believe." Widely acknowledged as Dickens's most autobiographical novel,* David Copperfield *has been much explored by psychologists.*

The "father" of psychoanalysis, Sigmund Freud, kept a copy of the novel in his consulting room and recommended it to friends and clients.

David Copperfield, published in 1849–50, contains some of Dickens's most-loved characters, including the Micawbers, Betsy Trotwood and the Peggotty family. There are also some of his most terrifying villains: Mr and Miss Murdstone, who torment David viciously in his childhood; the vengeful and deeply cruel Rosa Dartle; the unctuous and dangerous Uriah Heep; and the woundingly selfish James Steerforth, whose role in life is to seduce, hurt and betray.

The novel's many strands contain shocking themes and imagery, including alcoholism, domestic cruelty, prostitution and child abuse. That the book was so well received was a true measure of how popular Dickens had become. The brutality of some of the characters, and the pleasure they take in their own vindictiveness, continues to shock readers today.

Although Dickens's great friend and first biographer, John Forster, wrote after the author's death that "too much has been assumed" about the autobiographical nature of *David Copperfield*, Dickens wrote in a very telling letter to Forster when he was about to finish the novel: "... if I were to say even half of what *Copperfield* makes me feel tonight ... I should be turned inside out! I seem to be sending some part of myself into the Shadowy World." Dickens's daughter Katey was once asked if it was true she was her father's favourite child, to which she replied that the author's favourite child was David Copperfield.

ABOVE The inimitable Mr Micawber, an illustration by Joseph Clayton Clarke, who worked under the pseudonym "Kyd". At the end of *David Copperfield*, Mr Micawber and his family emigrate to Australia.

BELOW Little Em'ly, the orphaned niece of Daniel Peggotty, graces the title page of *David Copperfield*. When David sees her for the first time he describes Em'ly as "a most beautiful little girl".

Barkis Is Willin'

In *David Copperfield*, while the protagonist is still a child, he becomes the unwitting bearer of a declaration of love from the coach driver Barkis to Peggotty, David's devoted servant. Barkis asks David to include, when he writes to Peggotty, the message "Barkis is willin'" and the phrase became a popular quotation from the novel. Several decades later, Dickens's youngest son, Edward Bulwer Lytton Dickens, was an MP in New South Wales, Australia. During one parliamentary session, he was repeatedly interrupted by another MP, whose surname was Willis. As one newspaper reported the incident, "At last Mr Dickens stopped to remark, 'My father coined a famous phrase, "Barkis is willin'".' Under present circumstances I am strongly tempted to reverse it and say, "Willis is barking".' The house laughed and the interruptions ceased."

Charles Dickens was born on a Friday, a day he believed to be lucky and portentous in his life; he believed that beginning a new project on a Friday was a promising omen for its success. His belief was in direct contradiction with the popular superstition of the time, which claimed that Friday was an unlucky day (and Friday the 13th unluckiest of all). Dickens, however, believed that everything of import that had happened to him had taken place on a Friday; this belief was shaken when the Staplehurst train crash occurred on a Friday, but the fact that he and his companions were not killed reinforced his superstition.

Like the author, David Copperfield was born on a Friday. The narrator of his own life, David writes: "I record that I was born (as I have been informed and believe) on a Friday, at twelve o'clock at night. It was remarked that the clock began to strike, and I began to cry, simultaneously. In consideration of the day and hour of my birth, it was declared by the nurse ... that I was destined to be unlucky in life." Although in childhood he experiences more than his fair share of misery, as an adult, David is lucky and, eventually, happy and prosperous.

There are many parallels with Dickens's own life, including David's experience as a child labourer working for Murdstone and Grinby, the fact that David becomes a successful writer, and the character of Mr Micawber being so closely allied to Dickens's father's personality. There is also David's passion for his first wife Dora, analogous both to Dickens's early love for Maria Beadnell and the way in which his wife Catherine's "unsatisfactory" housekeeping skills were frustrating him by the time he wrote *David Copperfield*. There are, however, far more non-autobiographical elements to the story and although it can help readers to a partial understanding of the author's character, *David Copperfield* cannot be read as a true picture of Dickens's life and career.

22

DICKENS THE ACTOR

Charles Dickens's earliest career ambition was to make his name on the stage. His very first attempt at writing, at around the age of eight, had been a play named Miznar, The Sultan of India. *As an adolescent, the theatre continued to enthral him and he practised acting skills in his spare time; it has also been suggested that, out of his meagre wages as a legal clerk, he paid for acting lessons from the actor Robert Keeley.*

In early 1832, Dickens was offered an audition for a theatrical company owned by one of his heroes, the actor-manager Charles Mathews (1776–1835), at the Covent Garden Theatre. Mathews's comedy routines had made him one of the most popular faces on the London stage and he took his company on regular tours, both around Britain and to the USA. On the day of the audition, Dickens was suffering such a terrible cold that he was unable to get out of bed. Having missed his chance to audition, he reapplied for the following autumn, but by the time that autumn arrived, he was on his way to a successful career in writing, working for the *Morning Chronicle* (for which he wrote several theatrical reviews).

To feed his love of acting, Dickens took part in amateur theatricals. Together with his friends and siblings, he put on plays at John and Elizabeth Dickens's home in Bentinck Street, including a special family performance of the opera *Clari* in 1833. In 1834, Dickens wrote to his friend Henry Kolle about a burlesque he had written as a homage to Shakespeare, *O'Thello*. When Dickens met Catherine Hogarth, the couple discovered

they shared a great love of the theatre and throughout their early marriage, they often acted with friends in London. When they travelled to the USA and Canada in 1842, both Charles and Catherine performed onstage on several occasions. Dickens also often took charge of direction and stage management.

As the Dickens children grew up, their father began staging regular "family theatricals". These were not simple affairs and as each new theatrical was planned, it seemed to become more lavish than the last. Dickens would hire an army of workmen to turn the children's schoolroom into what he called "The Smallest Theatre in the World". The costumes were ordered from London's top theatrical costumier, Nathan's, and Dickens even hired a policeman to stand outside the house, check people's invitations and keep out gatecrashers.

Friends and other family members were also called upon to act, with names on the family theatrical playbills including Wilkie Collins, Augustus Egg, Mark Lemon and various members of the Hogarth family. A new theatrical would take over the family's life for several

ABOVE The original cast of *The Frozen Deep*, including members of the Dickens and Hogarth families, Mark Lemon (the first editor of *Punch*), the artist Augustus Egg and the novelist Wilkie Collins.

weeks: the house would be disrupted by the workmen and scene painters, the girls would be given regular coaching for their roles, and the boys would be sent their scripts at school and exhorted to learn all their lines before coming home for the holidays. Dickens loved the opportunity to work with his children and used the theatricals as a chance to let them shine. Henry later recalled being taken to see his father dressed up in his costume for a ghostly part, in order that he would not be frightened when Dickens appeared on stage. When the family put on *Tom Thumb*, Henry was so young and his voice so indistinct that the audience were given copies of his lines to enable them to follow what he was saying.

By the 1850s, Dickens was desperate to do more with his acting. He wanted to perform not just at home but in professional theatres with real audiences. In 1857, he staged *The Frozen Deep* – a play about an expedition to the Arctic, written by Wilkie Collins – at the Gallery of Illustration, a private theatre on London's Regent Street. With the play a huge success, the profits were given to the widow and family of the playwright Douglas Jerrold, a friend of Collins and Dickens who had died recently. Mrs Jerrold became quite angry at this very public display of charity, insisting that she did not need the money (although she probably did). Dickens, however, enjoyed basking in the glory that a public performance could bring, and he and Collins decided to take the production on tour to Manchester. The London performances starred the usual amateur troupe of members of the Dickens family and friends, and it was the search for professional actresses, to replace Dickens's daughters and sisters-in-law when they took the play on tour, that led Dickens to meet Ellen Ternan.

Towards the end of his life, Dickens's love of acting was fed by his hugely popular public reading tours. He did not just stand on the stage and read, he played all the parts, producing a wealth of voices and turning himself into each of the characters. Many

Private Theatricals.

STAGE MANAGER, MR. CHARLES DICKENS.

ON SATURDAY EVENING, APRIL 27, 1833,

At Seven o'clock precisely. The performances will commence with

AN INTRODUCTORY PROLOGUE;

THE PRINCIPAL CHARACTERS BY

MR. EDWARD BARROW; MR. MILTON; MR. CHARLES DICKENS; MISS AUSTIN;
AND MISS DICKENS.

IMMEDIATELY AFTER WHICH WILL BE PRESENTED THE OPERA OF

CLARI.

The Duke Vivaldi	MR. BRAMWELL,
Rolamo, a Farmer, (Father to Clari)	MR. C. DICKENS,
Jocoso, (Valet to the Duke)	MR. H. AUSTIN,
Nicolo	MR. MILTON,
Geronio	MR. E. BARROW,
Nimpedo	MR. R. AUSTIN,
Pages to the Duke	MASTERS F. DICKENS & A. DICKENS.
Clari	MISS DICKENS,
Fidalma (her Mother)	MISS L. DICKENS,
Vespina	MISS AUSTIN,
Ninette	MISS OPPENHEIM.

CHARACTERS IN THE EPISODE.

The Nobleman	MR. HENRY KOLLE.
Pelgrino, a Farmer	MR. JOHN DICKENS,
Wife of Pelgrino	MISS URQUHART,
Leoda	MISS OPPENHEIM.

AFTER WHICH THE FAVOURITE INTERLUDE OF

The Married Bachelor.

Sir Charles Courtall	MR. C. DICKENS,
Sharp	MR. JOHN URQUHART,
Lady Courtall	MISS L. DICKENS,
Grace	MISS DICKENS.

TO CONCLUDE WITH THE FARCE OF

Amateurs & Actors.

David Dulcet, Esq. (a Musical Dramatic Amateur, who employs Mr. O. P. Bustle, and attached to Theatricals and Miss Mary Hardacre) . . . MR. H. AUSTIN.

Mr. O. P. Bustle, (a Provincial Manager, but engaged to superintend some Private Theatricals) MR. BRAMWELL,

Wing (a poor Country Actor) . . . MR. C. DICKENS,

Berry, (an Actor for the heavy Business) . . . . MR. BOSTON.

Elderberry, (a retired Manufacturer, simple in wit and manners, and utterly unacquainted with Theatricals) . . . MR. J. DICKENS,

Timkins, (Elderberry's Factotum) MR. R. AUSTIN,

Geoffry Muffincap, (an elderly Charity Boy, let out as a Servant at Bustle's Lodging) . . MR. E. BARROW,

Miss Mary Hardacre, (a fugitive Ward of Elderberry's . . . MISS DICKENS,

Mrs. Mary Gunveil, (a Strolling Tragedy Actress, and a serious evil to her Husband) . . MISS OPPENHEIM

The Scenery by Messrs. H. Austin, Milton, H. Kolle, and Assistants.——The Band which will be numerous and complete, under the direction of Mr. E. Barrow.

J. & O. Nichols, Printers, Earl's Court, Cranbourn Street, Soho.

THE SMALLEST THEATRE IN THE WORLD!

TAVISTOCK HOUSE.

LESSEE AND MANAGER - - - MR. CRUMMLES.

On Tuesday Evening, June 19th, 1855, will be presented, AT EXACTLY EIGHT O'CLOCK,

AN ENTIRELY NEW AND ORIGINAL

DOMESTIC MELO-DRAMA, IN TWO ACTS, BY MR. WILKIE COLLINS,

NOW FIRST PERFORMED, CALLED

THE LIGHTHOUSE.

THE SCENERY PAINTED BY MR. STANFIELD, R.A.

AARON GURNOCK, the head Light-keeper	MR. CRUMMLES.
MARTIN GURNOCK, his son ; the second Light-keeper	MR. WILKIE COLLINS.
JACOB DALE, the third Light-keeper	MR. MARK LEMON.
SAMUEL FURLEY, a Pilot	MR. AUGUSTUS EGG, A.R.A.
THE RELIEF OF LIGHT-KEEPERS, BY MR. CHARLES DICKENS, JUNIOR, MR. EDWARD HOGARTH, MR. ALFRED AINGER, and MR. WILLIAM WEBSTER.	
THE SHIPWRECKED LADY	MISS HOGARTH.
PHŒBE	MISS DICKENS.

Who will sing a new Ballad, the Music by MR. LINLEY, the Words by MR. CRUMMLES, entitled

THE SONG OF THE WRECK.

I.
The wind blew high, the waters raved,
A Ship drove on the land,
A hundred human creatures saved,
Knelt down upon the sand.
Three-score were drowned, three-score were thrown
Upon the black rocks wild ;
And thus among them left alone,
They found one helpless child.

II.
A Seaman rough, to shipwreck bred,
Stood out from all the rest,
And gently held the lonely head
Upon his honest breast.
And trav'ling o'er the Desert wide,
It was a solemn joy
To see them, ever side by side,
The sailor and the boy.

III.
In famine, sickness, hunger, thirst,
The two were still but one,
Until the strong man droop'd the first,
And felt his labours done.
Then to a trusty friend he spake :
" Across this Desert wide
" O take the poor boy for my sake !"
And kissed the child, and died.

IV.
Toiling along in weary plight,
Through heavy jungle-mire,
Those two came later every night
To warm them at the fire,
Until the Captain said one day :
" O nameless good and kind,
" To save thyself now come away,
" And leave the boy behind !"

V.
The child was slumb'ring near the blaze :
" O Captain let him rest
" Until it sinks, when God's own ways
" Shall teach us what is best !"
They watched the whiten'd ashy heap,
They touched the child in vain,
They did not leave him there asleep,
He never woke again.

HALF-AN-HOUR FOR REFRESHMENT.

TO CONCLUDE WITH

The Guild Amateur-Company's Farce, in One Act, by MR. CRUMMLES and MR. MARK LEMON.

MR. NIGHTINGALE'S DIARY.

MR. NIGHTINGALE	MR. FRANK STONE, A.R.A.
MR. GABBLEWIG, of the Middle Temple	
CHARLEY BIT, a Boots	
MR. POULTER, a Pedestrian and Cold Water Drinker	MR. CRUMMLES.
CAPTAIN BLOWER, an Invalid	
A RESPECTABLE FEMALE	
A DEAF SEXTON	
TIP, Mr. Gabblewig's Tiger	MR. AUGUSTUS EGG, A.R.A.
CHRISTOPHER, a Charity Boy	
SLAP, Professionally Mr. Flormiville, a Country Actor	
MR. TICKLE, Inventor of the celebrated Compounds	MR. MARK LEMON.
A VIRTUOUS YOUNG PERSON IN THE CONFIDENCE OF MARIA	
LITHERS, Landlord of the Water Lily	MR. WILKIE COLLINS.
ROSINA, Mr. Nightingale's Niece	MISS KATE DICKENS.
SUSAN, her Maid	MISS HOGARTH.

Composer and Director of the Music, MR. FRANCESCO BERGER, who will Preside at the Piano-forte.
Costume Makers, MESSRS. NATHAN, of Titchbourne Street, Haymarket. Perruquier, MR. WILSON, of the Strand.
Machinery and Properties by MR. IRELAND, of the Theatre Royal, Adelphi.

DOORS OPEN AT HALF-PAST SEVEN. CARRIAGES MAY BE ORDERED AT A QUARTER-PAST ELEVEN.

ABOVE LEFT & RIGHT *Clari* and *The Lighthouse* playbills. The family theatricals were carefully managed by Charles Dickens, who oversaw every aspect of the performances. Attention was paid to every detail, such as the beautifully painted scenery, the professionally made costumes and playbills revealing who played each role.

OPPOSITE Playbill for a family theatrical held at Tavistock House of *The Frozen Deep*. Dickens would later meet his mistress, Ellen Ternan, when performing in a professional production of *The Frozen Deep*.

TAVISTOCK HOUSE THEATRE.

UNDER THE MANAGEMENT OF MR. CHARLES DICKENS.

On Wednesday, January 14th, 1857, AT A QUARTER BEFORE 8 O'CLOCK, will be presented

AN ENTIRELY NEW

ROMANTIC DRAMA, IN THREE ACTS, BY MR. WILKIE COLLINS,

CALLED

THE FROZEN DEEP.

The Machinery and Properties, by Mr. IRELAND, of the Theatre Royal, Adelphi. The Dresses by MESSRS. NATHAN, of Titchbourne Street, Haymarket. Perruquier, Mr. WILSON, of the Strand.

THE PROLOGUE WILL BE DELIVERED BY MR. JOHN FORSTER.

CAPTAIN EBSWORTH, *of The Sea Mew*	Mr. EDWARD PIGOTT.
CAPTAIN HELDING, *of The Wanderer*	Mr. ALFRED DICKENS.
LIEUTENANT CRAYFORD	Mr. MARK LEMON.
FRANK ALDERSLEY	Mr. WILKIE COLLINS.
RICHARD WARDOUR	Mr. CHARLES DICKENS.
LIEUTENANT STEVENTON	Mr. YOUNG CHARLES.
JOHN WANT, *Ship's Cook*	Mr. AUGUSTUS EGG, A.R.A.
BATESON ⎫ *Two of The Sea Mew's People*	⎧ Mr. EDWARD HOGARTH.
DARKER ⎭	⎩ Mr. FREDERICK EVANS.

(OFFICERS AND CREWS OF THE SEA MEW AND WANDERER.)

MRS. STEVENTON	Miss HELEN.
ROSE EBSWORTH	Miss KATE.
LUCY CRAYFORD	Miss HOGARTH.
CLARA BURNHA	Miss MARY.
NURSE ESTHER	Mrs. WILLS.
MAID	Miss MARTHA.

THE SCENERY AND SCENIC EFFECTS OF THE FIRST ACT, BY MR. TELBIN,
THE SCENERY AND SCENIC EFFECTS OF THE SECOND AND THIRD ACTS, BY **Mr. STANFIELD, R.A.**
ASSISTED BY MR. DANSON.
THE ACT-DROP, ALSO BY **Mr. STANFIELD, R.A.**

AT THE END OF THE PLAY, HALF-AN-HOUR FOR REFRESHMENT.

To Conclude with the Farce, in Two Acts, by Mr. BUCKSTONE, called

UNCLE JOHN.

UNCLE JOHN	Mr. CHARLES DICKENS.
NEPHEW HAWK	Mr. WILKIE COLLINS.
FRIEND THOMAS	Mr. MARK LEMON.
EDWARD EASEL	Mr. AUGUSTUS EGG, A.R.A.
ANDREW	Mr. YOUNG CHARLES.
NIECE HAWK	Miss HOGARTH.
ELIZA	Miss KATE.
MRS. COMFORT	Miss MARY.

Musical Composer and Conductor of the Orchestra—Mr. FRANCESCO BERGER, who will preside at the Piano.

CARRIAGES MAY BE ORDERED AT HALF-PAST ELEVEN.

GOD SAVE THE QUEEN!

years later, in her book about her father, Mamie recalled a scene from her childhood when she was ill and spent the day sleeping on a sofa in his study. She woke up frightened by hearing voices in the room, only to see her father standing in front of the mirror acting out his latest chapter. He acted each role so he could be sure he would write natural-sounding dialogue, and to let him work out what facial expressions his characters would have had while speaking the words. It was this knowledge of acting and characterization that allows Dickens's novels to be so easily adapted to the stage and screen today.

ABOVE This engraving is of an 1846 painting by CR Leslie. It shows Dickens in one of his favourite roles, as Captain Bobadil in Ben Johnson's play *Every Man in his Humour.*

LEFT Mark Lemon (1809–70) was a regular and welcome visitor to the Dickens household. In 1848 he published a fairytale, *The Enchanted Doll*, which he dedicated to "Mary and Kate Dickens".

OPPOSITE Visiting cards; after the advent of photography, the Victorian calling card became more elaborate and personalized. Charles Dickens's visiting cards show the author as he wished to be viewed by his friends and business acquaintances.

MASON & Cᵒ   28 OLD BOND STREET

JOHN & CHARLES WATKINS, PHOT

23

MAGAZINES: HOUSEHOLD WORDS & ALL THE YEAR ROUND

Dickens worked on a number of magazines, as a writer and an editor, including Bentley's Miscellany *and* Master Humphrey's Clock.

But the two most famous titles are those he spearheaded: *Household Words* and *All the Year Round*.

Household Words was set up in 1850. It was published by the firm of Bradbury & Evans but, as was promised in the advertising, it was "conducted by Mr Charles Dickens". Dickens had become frustrated by not having autonomy on the magazines and newspapers he had worked on previously and he longed to have the final say about content and style. Bradbury & Evans provided the financial backing, while Dickens provided the editorship and the celebrity to get the magazine off the press and into people's homes. It was intended "for the Entertainment and Instruction of all classes of readers" and promised to promote discussion of "the most important social questions" of the era. Dickens was enthused by the idea; he wrote celebratory letters to friends, wooed writers and waxed lyrical about the philosophies he saw the magazine embodying. "We hope to do some solid good,"

he wrote to one friend, adding that he wanted to expose "all social evils".

Despite Dickens's fervour, by the end of 1853, *Household Words* was struggling. The initial interest from the public had begun to dissipate and Dickens realized he needed a new and exciting formula to make people start buying it again. His solution was to publish his new novel, *Hard Times*, as a serial in the magazine. The first episode appeared in April 1854; within three months the number of issues being sold had doubled.

By the end of the decade, Dickens was fed up with *Household Words*; he was also restless, sad and guilt-laden after ending his marriage and from falling out spectacularly with so many friends over matters both personal and literary. He wanted a new challenge and he wanted to be out of his contract with Bradbury & Evans. Courting controversy once again, he began wooing new contacts and went into partnership with Chapman & Hall.

On 28 May 1859, the very last issue of *Household Words* was published, coinciding with an edition of Dickens's newest project, the rival magazine *All the Year Round*. Playing safe, he had already released a few issues of this new magazine before bringing about the demise of *Household Words*. In contrast to his editorship of the previous title, Dickens wrote very few articles for *All the Year Round*, preferring to concentrate on serializing his novels and on finding other contributors. *All the Year Round* began in grand style with the weekly serialization of *A Tale of Two Cities*. This exciting historical novel, set during the French Revolution and encapsulating Dickens's style, captured the public's imagination and ensured the success of the author's latest venture.

Dickens was adept at discovering new literary talent, encouraging new writers and giving work to many of his friends. He always paid good wages – something

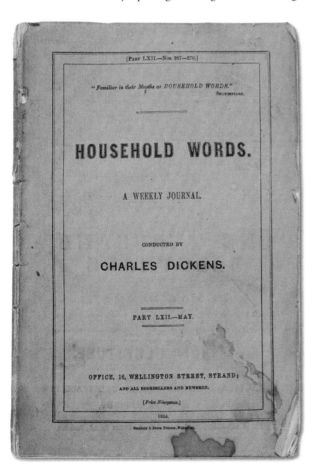

Unorthodox Friends: Wilkie Collins and Count d'Orsay

The novelist Wilkie Collins met Charles Dickens for the first time in 1851; they became instant friends, recognizing in each other an unconventionality Dickens could not reveal in most aspects of his life. The two men regularly went travelling together and collaborated on joint writing projects, including *The Lazy Tour of Two Idle Apprentices* (1857). With Collins, Dickens could relax and behave in a more scandalous fashion than he could with more straight-laced friends such as John Forster.

Another friend with whom Dickens could indulge his wild side was Count d'Orsay, the flamboyant, amusing and bisexual lover of the philanthropic Lady Blessington. D'Orsay was not only Lady Blessington's lover, he had also been unhappily married to her stepdaughter, Lady Harriet Gardiner (in a court case to dissolve the marriage, Harriet had agreed to pay more than £100,000 towards her husband's debts). The two men met at Lady Blessington's home, Gore House, and d'Orsay became a friend of the Dickens family; he was asked, along with the poet Alfred, Lord Tennyson, to be godfather to Charles and Catherine's son Alfred.

OPPOSITE Pencil portrait of Alfred Guillaume Gabriel, Count d'Orsay (1801–52) by Jean-Baptiste Isabey. D'Orsay grew up in France but moved to London in 1830, where he became close friends with Dickens and his family.

LEFT With *Household Words* – whose cover is seen here – Dickens enjoyed editorial autonomy. He hoped fervently that the articles would help to expose, and thereby end, "all social evils".

The Daily News.

No. 1.   LONDON, WEDNESDAY, JANUARY 21, 1846.   PRICE 5d.

RIGHT Wilkie Collins (1824–89) was a close friend and literary collaborator of Dickens. This portrait was painted in 1853 by Wilkie's younger brother Charles Alston Collins (1828–73), the first husband of Katey Dickens.

OPPOSITE The first edition of the *Daily News*, 21 January 1846. Dickens set up this radical newspaper to directly compete with the *Morning Chronicle*. Dickens edited the first 17 issues, but stepped aside in favour of his friend John Forster, as he couldn't afford the time such a role required. In 1930, it was absorbed into the *Daily Chronicle*, which closed in 1960.

few magazine editors did. The famous writers whose work appeared in Dickens's magazines include William Makepeace Thackeray, Wilkie Collins, Elizabeth Gaskell, Elizabeth Barrett Browning, Leigh Hunt, George Augustus Sala and Harriet Martineau. Dickens sought out the work of Mrs Gaskell and, when critics were angered by a woman writing about such subjects as illegitimacy and suicide, encouraged her to keep writing the truth about Victorian society. He spent years trying to persuade George Eliot to write for his magazines, but she refused.

Another writer whom Dickens took under his wing was Charles Allston Collins ("Charlie"), the younger brother of Wilkie Collins and husband of Katey. Charlie Collins was a very talented artist who gave up painting in order to write; his father-in-law gave him regular work despite the fact Charlie had little of his older brother's literary skills. One of the reasons Dickens championed Charlie as a writer was guilt – it was largely Dickens's fault, because of his furious criticism of Pre-Raphaelite art, that Charlie Collins had stopped being an artist and had chosen to concentrate on writing instead.

24

BLEAK HOUSE

The first words of Bleak House *were written at Tavistock House in London, in November 1851, just after the Dickenses moved into their new home – a larger house leased in keeping with their growing numbers and income. The novel was not completed until August 1853, while Dickens and his family were on holiday in one of his favourite places, Boulogne, in France.*

It forms one of Dickens's most scathing commentaries on the British legal system. The first chapter, entitled "In Chancery", begins with a superbly atmospheric description of London in the grip of a dense and choking fog. This "implacable November weather" was also a metaphor for the impenetrability of the legal system, with its twists and turns that kept people gripped forever in a mire of indecipherable language and hard-to-define clauses and conditions. Through his early career experience as a clerk in Doctor's Commons, Dickens had become acquainted with court cases as convoluted and frustrating as his fictional case of Jarndyce v Jarndyce (the lynchpin of this novel) and the idea for *Bleak House* had been germinating for many years.

The story begins in Lincoln's Inn in London, not far from Dickens's first adult home at Furnival's Inn, and throughout the novel, the reader is constantly reminded of this world of law courts and solicitors' offices. The enormous cast of characters is made up of people connected, in some way, with the Jarndyce family and the case, even if the characters themselves are unaware of the connection.

Bleak House switches between different characters' perspectives and narratives, the most prominent narrative being that of Esther Summerson. Dickens was courting controversy by choosing an illegitimate child – and a girl – as his heroine. Esther is one of several characters throughout Dickens's novels whom he uses to challenge the prevailing Victorian psyche. Through characters such as Esther and Oliver Twist, he was trying to make his readers aware that illegitimate children should not be shunned or treated cruelly for circumstances beyond their control.

Another of *Bleak House*'s most unforgettable characters is Jo the crossing sweeper, a child labourer forced into poverty and who is near starvation almost every day of his miserable existence. Dickens chose Jo's profession carefully: his readers would all be used to seeing crossing sweepers, would expect them to clear a path through the mud and dirt to keep their fine clothes clean, but few of his readers would ever have thought before that they should care about the lives of the people who swept a path before them.

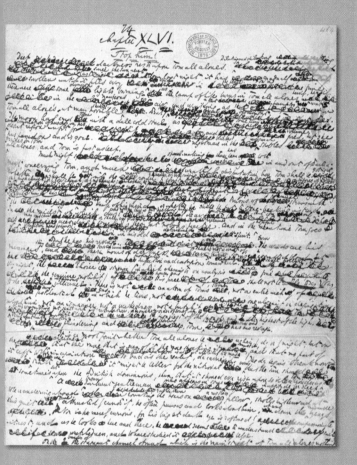

"You do not think he is ill?" said I.

No. He looked robust in body.

"That he cannot be at peace in mind, we have too much reason to know," I proceeded. "Mr. Woodcourt, you are going to London?"

"To-morrow or the next day."

"There is nothing Richard wants so much as a friend. He always liked you. Pray see him when you get there. Pray help him sometimes with your companionship, if you can. You do not know of what service it might be. You cannot think how Ada, and Mr. Jarndyce, and even I —how we should all thank you, Mr. Woodcourt!"

"Miss Summerson," he said, and seemed more moved than he had been from the first, "before Heaven, I will be a true friend to him! I will accept him as a trust, and it shall be a sacred one!"

"God bless you!" said I, with my eyes filling fast; but I thought they might, when it was not for myself. "Ada loves him—we all love him, but Ada loves him as we cannot. I will tell her what you say. Thank you, and God bless you, in her name!"

Richard came back as we finished changing these hurried words, and gave me his arm to take me to the coach.

"Woodcourt," he said, unconscious with what application, "let us meet in London!"

"Meet?" returned the other. "I have scarcely a friend there, but now, your—where shall I find you?"

"Why, I must get a lodging of some sort," said Richard, pondering. "Say at Vholes's, Symond's Inn."

"Good! Without loss of time."

They shook hands heartily. When I was seated in the coach, and Richard was yet standing in the street, Mr. Woodcourt laid his hand upon his shoulder, and looked at me. I understood him, and waved mine in thanks.

And in his last look as we drove away, I saw that he was sorry for me. I was glad to see it. I felt for my old self as the dead may feel if they ever revisit these scenes. I was glad to be tenderly remembered, to be gently pitied, not to be quite forgotten.

CHAPTER XLVI.

Stop him!

Darkness rests upon Tom-all-alone's. Dilating and dilating since the sun went down last night, it has gradually swollen until it fills every void in the place. For a time there were some dungeon lights burning as the lamp of Life burns in Tom-all-alone's, heavily, heavily, in the nauseous air, and winking—as that lamp, too, winks in Tom-all-alone's—at many horrible things. But they are blotted out. The moon has eyed Tom with a dull cold stare, as admitting some puny emulation of herself in his desert region unfit for life and blasted by volcanic fires; but she has passed on, and is gone. The blackest nightmare in the infernal stables grazes on Tom-all-alone's, and Tom is fast asleep.

ABOVE LEFT & RIGHT Two pages of *Bleak House* showing the evolution of Dickens's manuscripts. Both show the same page, from Chapter XLVI. One is a heavily corrected page from the handwritten manuscript. The other has been typeset and shows a few corrections in Dickens's handwriting.

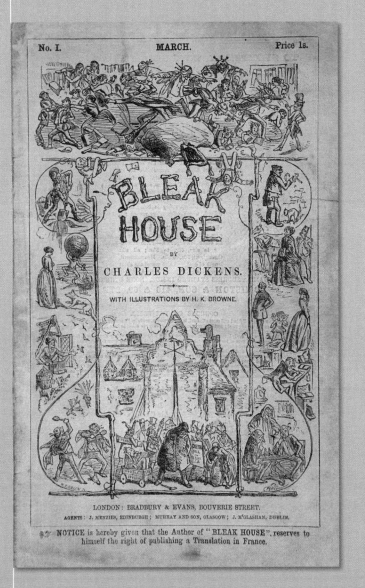

Miss Jellyby.

ABOVE LEFT & RIGHT *Bleak House* monthly edition, an extract from the March edition. The novel is a brilliant, convoluted satire about the legal system, inspired by Dickens's early career in the legal world. This edition was illustrated by Hablot Knight Browne – better known as Phiz.

Bleak House is also notable for Dickens's foray into the world of detective fiction. One enticing strand of the novel follows the search for a murderer, and the man in charge of the case is Inspector Bucket, who was largely modelled on Dickens's friend Inspector Field. Crime fiction was a new genre and Dickens's interest was piqued by the work of his friend and collaborator Wilkie Collins, whose novels include *The Moonstone* and *The Woman in White*.

The raw afternoon is rawest, and the dense fog is densest, and the muddy streets are muddiest near that leaden-headed old obstruction, appropriate ornament for the threshold of a leaden-headed old corporation, Temple Bar. And hard by Temple Bar, in Lincoln's Inn Hall, at the very heart of the fog, sits the Lord High Chancellor in his High Court of Chancery.

BLEAK HOUSE

ABOVE Dickens spent many summers in Broadstairs, and wrote many of his books here. The Albion Hotel is mentioned in his article 'Our English Watering Place'. They also stayed at nearby Fort House, now renamed Bleak House.

DICKENS AND DETECTIVES

When Charles Dickens was seven years old, Robert Peel — leader of the Tory party and later to become prime minister — founded the Metropolitan Police Force. It was London's first effective police department.

In 1842, when the name of Charles Dickens was as famous as that of Sir Robert Peel, the city's first Detective Department was formed.

The police and detectives feature several times in Dickens's fiction, from his early irreverent portrayals of bumbling policemen through to psychologically fascinating creations of admirable detectives. During Dickens's career, the public's perception of the efficacy of the police underwent a great change, and Dickens's writing reflects this. In 1830s London, the bobby on the beat was not revered and policemen were often seen as figures of fun. This was epitomized by Dickens in his portrayal of the incompetent, unintelligent duo of Blathers and Duff, the officers who are sent to investigate the robbery in *Oliver Twist*, but who are far more interested in sampling the Maylies' drinks cupboard than in solving the crime. Dickens also emphasizes the excruciatingly obvious class difference between the policemen and the family they have been sent to protect: *"This is the lady of the house," said Mr Losberne, motioning towards Mrs Maylie. Mr Blathers made a bow. Being desired to sit down, he put his hat on the floor, and taking a chair,* motioned Duff to do the same. The latter gentleman, who did not appear quite so much accustomed to good society, or quite so much at his ease in it – one of the two – seated himself, after undergoing several muscular affections of the limbs, and forced the head of his stick into his mouth, with some embarrassment.

In *Martin Chuzzlewit*, written after the formation of the Detective Department, Dickens created his first true detective, Mr Nadgett: "he was born to be a secret ... How he lived was a secret; where he lived was a secret; and even what he was, was a secret." Throughout the novel, Dickens made it his mission to keep Nadgett's discoveries and the contents of his notes a guarded secret from the reader as well as from the detective's quarry. It is a wonderful psychological portrait not only of a detective but also of the effects Nadgett's presence has on all those around him. Dickens was not alone in creating what is now known as some of the earliest detective fiction. His great friend Wilkie Collins published his detective novel *The Moonstone* in 1868, and Dickens declared it to be his friend's best novel so far: "much better than anything he has done [before]".

ABOVE During his time as home secretary, Robert Peel (1788–1850) made it his mission to create an effective police force. His name gave rise to the police nicknames "bobbies" and "peelers".

ABOVE Henry Fielding (1707–54), novelist, dramatist, magistrate and reformer. In 1749, he founded the Bow Street Runners, London's first police force. Dickens named his eighth child Henry Fielding Dickens.

The Real Inspector Bucket

Inspector Charles Field (1805–74) joined the Metropolitan Police as soon as it was founded and became one of its first detectives in 1842. Four years later he was appointed chief of the Detective Division. Field met Charles Dickens for the first time in the 1840s; the celebrated detective and the celebrated author had a great deal in common, not least the discovery of a shared early ambition to become an actor. One of Field's most notable characteristics while talking was to punctuate important points by jabbing his face or the air with his forefinger. Dickens attributed this characteristic to his fictional detective, whom Mr Snagsby describes as "Mr Bucket with his forefinger, and his confidential manner impossible to be evaded or declined". After retiring in 1852, Inspector Field became a private investigator, something that was frowned upon by the establishment. Ironically, his detective involvement in high-profile cases led to Field being investigated by his own former police force.

It was perhaps as a direct consequence of *The Moonstone* that Dickens decided to write *The Mystery of Edwin Drood*; by an accident of fate, his last novel turned out to be the best mystery ever written. Edwin Drood disappears mysteriously one Christmas Eve – but what has happened to him? Has a murder been committed, as the reader is intended to believe? If so, who is the murderer? Because Dickens died during the writing of the novel, leaving no indication of his intentions for the plot, generations of readers have pored over the unfinished *Mystery of Edwin Drood* in the hopes of being able to discern what would have happened. Films, books and television series have attempted to conclude Dickens's unfinished detective story, but the true intention of the author will always remain a mystery.

The most memorable detective in Dickens's fiction is Inspector Bucket, who appears in *Bleak House* and is charged with seeking out a murderer. Bucket's personality and methods of working were inspired by Dickens's friendship with the real-life police detective Inspector Charles Field. Bucket is liked and respected – even if grudgingly – by the rest of Dickens's characters, and the reader immediately feels him to be trustworthy: "He is a sharp-eyed man – a quick keen man – and he takes in everybody's look at

The Murder at Road Hill House

In this much-discussed case of a murdered child, Dickens was convinced that the boy's father, Samuel Kent, and nurse had together killed him, then mutilated and disposed of the body. He wrote to a friend in Switzerland in February 1861:

> *You talk of the Road Murder, I suppose, even at Lausanne? Not all the Detective Police in existence shall ever persuade me out of the hypothesis that the circumstances have gradually shaped out to me mind. The father was in bed with the nurse: the child was discovered by them, sitting up in his little bed, staring, and evidently going to "tell Ma". The nurse leaped out of bed and instantly suffocated him in the father's presence. The father cut the child about, to distract suspicion (which was effectually done), and took the body out to where it was found. Either when he was going for the Police, or when he locked the police up in his own house, or at both times, he got rid of the knife and so forth. It is likely enough that the truth may never be discovered now.*

Although the child's half-sister Constance later confessed to the murder, it was believed she had done so in order to shield another and the case was never closed.

ABOVE Constance Kent at the "Road Hill Murder" trial of 1865, five years after the crime took place. She confessed to killing her half-brother in one of Victorian England's most notorious murder cases. Dickens believed her innocent.

him, all at once, individually and collectively, in a manner that stamps him a remarkable man..." Inspector Bucket moves with confidence in all areas of society and amongst every social class, whether the person he is questioning is an effronted baronet or a distressed child of the streets. Mrs Bucket also sleuths on her husband's behalf and has often been described as "the first Miss Marple".

Dickens was seduced by the idea of crime and, as he made explicit in his 1869 article "On an Amateur Beat", considered that in an alternative career he would have made a very good detective: "There is many a ruffian on the streets whom I mentally collar ... [he] would see mighty little of London ... if I could deal with him physically." In the cause of researching articles, he found himself accompanying detectives to some of the most dangerous areas of London. He followed avidly newspaper accounts of real murders and the bringing to justice of murderers; he attended magistrates' courts and widely discussed the causes célèbres of his time with his friends. Dickens's short story "Hunted Down" was based on the exploits of the notorious poisoner Thomas Griffiths Wainewright, who died in 1847. The author was also fascinated by the sensational Road Hill House case of 1860 – in which a little boy disappeared from his home and was later discovered murdered – that gripped the British public and was discussed widely all over the country for some years.

In 1868, during his second visit to the USA, Dickens heard the story of a murder that had taken place in Boston in the 1840s. Dr George Parkman disappeared in November 1849. Shortly afterwards, his burned corpse was discovered in a laboratory at Harvard University; Professor John Webster, Professor of Chemistry, was arrested and later hanged. Dickens took great pains to find out everything he could about the case and used elements of the story as inspiration for *The Mystery of Edwin Drood*. Edwin disappears as suddenly and mysteriously as Parkman had done. Following his disappearance, his watch is found in the river; Webster, who had owed money to Parkman, had also disposed of his victim's watch in the river.

In addition to his fictional detectives, Dickens also wrote several articles for *Household Words* about his real-life experiences of going on patrol with the police. These included "A Detective Police Party" (1850; published

in two parts), "On Duty with Inspector Field" (1851) and "Down With the Tide" (1853), about working at night with the River Police. The articles all praise the police and their methods, but "A Detective Police Party" ends on an amusingly wry note: "one other circumstance finally wound up the evening, after our Detective guests had left us. One of the sharpest among them ... had his pocket picked, going home!"

ABOVE *A Pickpocket In Custody*, an 1836 illustration by George Cruikshank from *Sketches by Boz*. It shows the new "peelers", or London police force, in operation.

OPPOSITE TOP An 1883 illustration for *The Moonstone* by Wilkie Collins, which features the wily and intelligent detective Sergeant Cuff. Here Cuff is shown searching for evidence.

26

HARD TIMES

The shortest of Dickens's novels, Hard Times *was the first of his books to be serialized in the new magazine* Household Words, *in 1854. The setting is Coketown, an industrial town in the north of England, where the retired and wealthy merchant Thomas Gradgrind holds sway. Dickens tells us that Gradgrind's mouth was "wide, thin, and hard set" and his voice "inflexible, dry, and dictatorial".*

Gradgrind drums into his own children, and the children of the town, his fervently held belief that nothing in life is more important than facts. As he orders the schoolteacher, "Teach these boys and girls nothing but Facts... Plant nothing else, and root out everything else." As he is the financial benefactor of the school, his rules hold dominion over everyone else.

Gradgrind is furious to discover that two of his own children, Tom and Louisa, have become friends with Sissy Jupe, a child from the circus, and are fascinated by her life. When Sissy's father disappears, Gradgrind offers her a home – on the proviso that she breaks all ties with the circus. Alongside the Gradgrinds and the world of the circus, *Hard Times* is the story of Stephen Blackpool, an impoverished loom worker in the mill owned by Josiah Bounderby, who also owns the town's bank. Stephen's lot in life is to be mistreated by those who are richer, crueller or more devious than he and to be confined to "the hardest working part of Coketown, in the innermost fortifications of that ugly citadel, where Nature was as strongly bricked out as killing airs

and gases were bricked in". Stephen, who looks much older than his 40 years – "he had had a hard life" – is in love with Rachel, a good, kind woman who is also in love with him. Unfortunately, Stephen is already married, to an abusive alcoholic. He seeks advice about divorce, but is told the idea is impossible.

In January 1854, Dickens had visited Preston in Lancashire, which was in the throes of a seven-month strike by textile workers. The strike crippled the Lancashire cotton industry, as employers and workers fought a bitter battle about working conditions and pay. The strikers and their families suffered terrible privations. Just as Dickens had been inspired, in 1843, to write *A Christmas Carol* after witnessing grinding poverty in Manchester, the story of the Preston workers' plight inspired him to "strike the heaviest blow in my power" in favour of industrial labourers.

Although he penned most of *Hard Times* in London, the final episodes were written in Boulogne in France. Dickens had taken his first holiday in Boulogne in the summer of 1852, accompanied by his wife and

sister-in-law. The following summer, they took the whole family and lived in a chateau for several months. They returned in the summers of 1854 (when he was finishing *Hard Times*) and 1856, and Dickens sent several of his sons to a boarding school in Boulogne. After his separation from Catherine, Dickens and his mistress Ellen Ternan would also often spend time in the area.

Dickens wrote the whole of *Hard Times* in just seven months. It was a process which exhausted and depressed him and left him feeling "three parts mad, and the fourth delirious". The novel is a masterpiece of social commentary in the manner of Mrs Gaskell, but it is not an uplifting novel; unlike in the majority of Dickens's works, there is no happy ending for many of the residents of Coketown.

The serialization of the novel sold well, more than doubling the circulation of *Household Words*, but although Dickens's readers showed their approval, there were many who did not. The politician Lord Macaulay described the tone of the book as being "sullen Socialism". GK Chesterton wrote that *Hard Times* was "the expression of a righteous indignation ... It is perhaps the only place where Dickens, in defending happiness, for a moment forgets to be happy."

ABOVE A Victorian circus of the 1870s. Sissy Jupe's father is a clown in Sleary's Circus; early in the novel he disappears, and Sissy is told she must forget all about the circus.

27

DICKENS AND ARTISTS

*In nineteenth-century London, the worlds of literature and art were
closely linked. Dickens collected art and read artistic reviews,
and many of his friends were artists. These friends included Frank
Stone, who illustrated some of Dickens's writing and was also
a neighbour at Tavistock House.*

After Frank's early death, his son Marcus, also an artist, became even closer to the Dickens family. Marcus and Katey were very close in age; they painted together, encouraged one another and moved in the same artistic circles.

Dickens worked very closely with his illustrators, including Hablot Knight Browne, otherwise known as "Phiz", George Cattermole (1800–68), Fred Walker (1840–75), Luke Fildes (1843–1927), John Leech (1817–64) and George Cruikshank (1792–1878). Charles Allston Collins, Katey's first husband, worked on illustrations for *The Mystery of Edwin Drood*. Dickens was not happy with them and Collins was unable to complete the drawings through illness (which was later diagnosed as stomach cancer).

The friendship between George Cruikshank and Dickens began to cool after Cruikshank, the son of an alcoholic, became more actively involved with the Temperance movement; Dickens, who enjoyed drinking, disliked what he saw as Cruikshank's preaching.

The artist saw himself as a modern-day Hogarth and produced very popular works warning of the evils of alcohol, including *The Bottle* (1847) and *The Drunkard's Children* (1848). After Dickens wrote an unfavourable review of the latter – criticizing its philosophy but not its artistic merit – the friendship between the two men was never truly repaired. In 1871, Cruikshank claimed publicly that Dickens had stolen his ideas for the plot of *Oliver Twist*; it is worth noting that Cruikshank waited until after Dickens's death before making the claim.

LEFT This painting of Katey Dickens is by Marcus Stone (1840–1921), one of her good friends. Marcus's first teacher was his father, Frank Stone (1800–59), one of Dickens's illustrators and friends.

OPPOSITE William Powell Frith painted this portrait of Charles Dickens in 1859. Outwardly conventional, Frith was actually one of Dickens's most free-thinking friends.

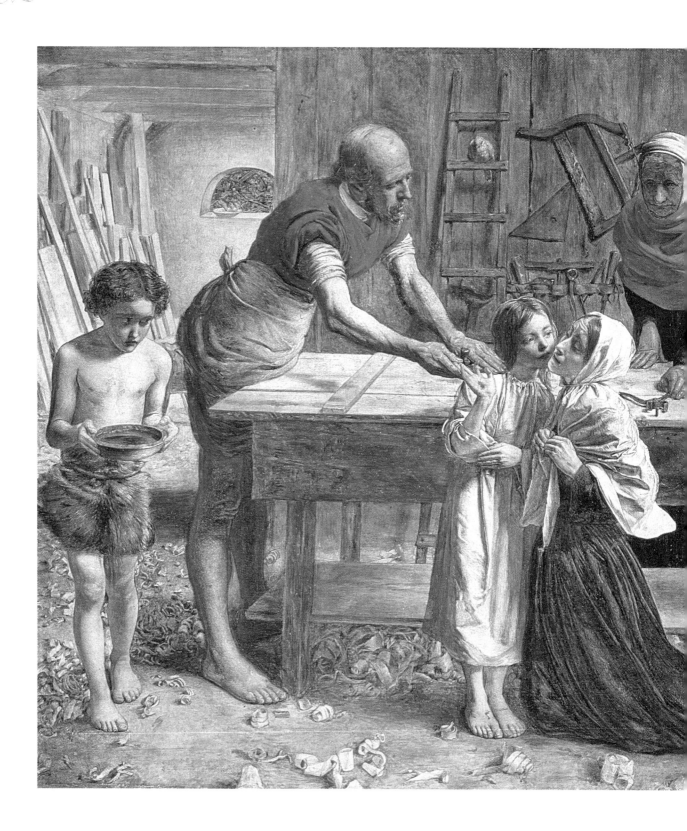

Turner's The Fighting Temeraire

While Dickens was working on *Nicholas Nickleby*, the artist Joseph Mallord William Turner (1775–1851) was painting one of his masterpieces, *The Fighting Temeraire Tugged to her Last Berth to be Broken Up*. It was exhibited at the Royal Academy in London in 1839; William Makepeace Thackeray, in a review of the exhibition, declared that seeing this one painting made the entrance fee worth paying. In 1855, Dickens commissioned Clarkson Stanfield to paint him a copy of Turner's masterpiece. The finished work was given pride of place on the wall at Dickens's home in Gad's Hill Place and can be seen in photographs of the house taken during the author's lifetime.

LEFT John Everett Millais's *Christ in the House of His Parents* (also known as *Christ in the Carpenter's Shop*) of 1849–50 was savagely criticized, not only by Dickens, because of the artist's decision to paint the holy family as working-class and non-romanticized.

Other artists in Dickens's circle included Clarkson Stanfield and Augustus Egg (1816–63), both of whom played essential parts in the Dickens family theatricals. In addition to acting, they produced elaborate backdrops and painted scenery for the stage. Several of Dickens's artist friends painted portraits of the writer, including Augustus Egg, Samuel Laurence (1812–84), William Powell Frith (1819–1909) and Daniel Maclise. Maclise's portrait from 1839 is one of the best-known images of a young Dickens; it was reproduced alongside the last episode of *Nicholas Nickleby* and has become known as "the Nickleby portrait". Dickens, who was never particularly keen on portraits of himself, wrote of the painting, "Maclise has made another face of me, which all people say is astonishing."

Dickens and the Pre-Raphaelites

One of the most famous artistic rows of the mid-nineteenth century centred around Charles Dickens and a newly formed artistic group, the Pre-Raphaelite Brotherhood. The group was founded in 1848 by John Everett Millais (1829–96), William Holman Hunt (1827–1910) and Dante

Gabriel Rossetti (1828–82). The three founding members of the Brotherhood – also known as the PRB – had studied at the Royal Academy. Having grown disenchanted with the Academy's style of teaching, the seven young 'Brothers' strove to change the course of British art – which they duly did. The PRB was a secret society, its ideals and aims known only to the group and their closest friends, which included Charles Allston Collins. When one of their friends got drunk at a party and inadvertently told the secret to a journalist, the newspapers had a field day. Dickens was so appalled by what he perceived as the overweening arrogance of the seven young men that he published a scathing article in *Household Words*, "New Lamps for Old Ones", deriding the new group and warning his readers against this "mean, odious, repulsive and revolting" school of art.

The painting that came in for most of his fury was Millais's *Christ in the House of His Parents*. Dickens was angered by Millais's depiction of Jesus as the child of poor, labouring parents. The author described the child in the painting as "a hideous, wry-necked, blubbering, red-headed boy, in a bed-gown, who appears to have received a poke in the hand, from the stick of another boy with whom he has been playing in an adjacent gutter". The artist's Virgin Mary was "a kneeling woman, so horrible in her ugliness, that (supposing it were possible for any human creature to exist for a moment with that dislocated throat) she would stand out from the rest of the company as a Monster, in the vilest cabaret in France, or the lowest ginshop in England."

Many years later, Katey revealed that her father had come to regret his furious criticism of the Pre-Raphaelites. Dickens's words were so influential that an enormous public backlash had ensued, blighting the careers of many struggling artists, including artists with no connection to the group who painted in a similar style. A few years after Dickens's article was published, he was introduced to Millais by a mutual friend – the two men got on extremely well. Some time later, the artist asked Dickens's permission to paint Katey for what would become one of his most popular paintings, *The Black Brunswicker*. In 1903, Katey wrote an article for *The Magazine of Art* entitled "Charles Dickens as a Lover of Art and Artists". It was described in the *New York Times* as "authoritative chapters on the life and character of Charles Dickens", including "reminiscences, anecdotes, and illustrations".

ABOVE Katey Dickens was the model for the young woman in *The Black Brunswicker* (1860) by John Everett Millais. It was painted during her engagement to Millais's good friend, Charles Allston Collins.

OPPOSITE TOP *The Boy Gambles his Money* (1848) is part of George Cruikshank's series *The Drunkard's Children*. Dickens and Cruikshank fell out over the illustrator's strong support of the Temperance movement.

OPPOSITE BOTTOM This photograph of John Everett Millais was taken at the artist's home in July 1865. The photographer was Charles Lutwidge Dodgson, better known by his pen name of Lewis Carroll.

28

LIVING IN PARIS

*In 1855, with their two daughters approaching marriageable age,
Charles and Catherine Dickens decided to spend several months
living in Paris. Charles was a Francophile who had visited
Paris several times already and he loved to take his family
on holiday to Boulogne.*

It was not easy to find suitable accommodation because, in 1855, Paris was hosting the Exposition Universelle. The spectacle, modelled on London's Great Exhibition of 1851, made Paris the fashionable destination for a vast swarm of tourists. A large area of the city was turned into the Palais de l'Industrie, in which exhibitors from 34 nations showcased their talents.

The family travelled to France in mid-October 1855. Knowing accommodation would be scarce, Charles and Georgina Hogarth left Catherine and the children in a comfortable hotel in Boulogne and went to Paris with just a couple of servants. They stayed in a hotel while house-hunting and became frustrated by how difficult it was to find a home for the family. Eventually they settled for 49 Avenue des Champs-Elysées, which was smaller than they had hoped for, but in a perfect location. Charles wrote to his wife that she should prepare herself for "a regular continental abode ... the view

is delightfully cheerful. I think the situation itself, almost the finest in Paris." To his friend and editor WH Wills, he wrote: "You must picture it as the smallest place you ever saw, but as exquisitely cheerful and vivacious ... and with a moving panorama always outside."

Although the Dickens boys were away at school, they came to Paris for the holidays. As Charles wrote to Edmund Yates, "on Christmas Day, I had seven sons in the Banquet Hall of this apartment – which would not make a very large warm bath." Katey and Mamie were in Paris to be "finished". They continued their

LEFT The Dickens family lived in this building, 49 Avenue des Champs-Elysées, in the heart of Paris.

OPPOSITE A French caricature of Charles Dickens standing astride the English Channel, with one foot in London and the other in Paris.

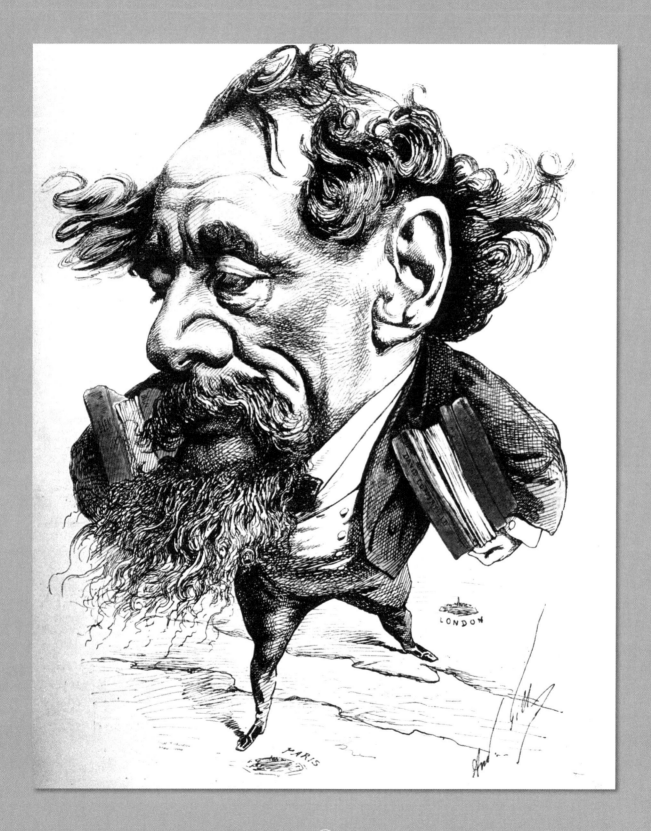

LONDON

PARIS

lessons, learned new styles of dancing, bought clothes in the latest fashions and perfected their French. They also continued studying Italian, a language both girls had learned in Genoa, under the tutelage of the exiled revolutionary leader Daniele Manin (who had been forced to flee his native Venice). Mamie and Katey shared their art lessons with the daughters of William Makepeace Thackeray, who were staying in Paris with their grandparents.

The family's months in Paris were a whirl of social events, fine restaurants and exciting new acquaintances. Dickens was as famous in France as he was in England, and he was introduced to the glitterati of Paris, including George Sand, Emile de Girardin and soprano Pauline Viardot, the lover of both the artist Ary Scheffer and the celebrated Russian novelist Ivan Turgenev. Dickens missed meeting Turgenev and his compatriot Leo Tolstoy, both of whom arrived in Paris within months of Dickens leaving it.

OPPOSITE A magic-lantern slide showing a view of the Champs-Elysées and the Arc de Triomphe as they looked in 1856.

RIGHT This sketch shows Dickens leaving the Paris morgue, which was, at the time of his visit, a tourist attraction. Dickens found the idea repellant, yet he visited on several occasions when seeking inspiration.

BELOW RIGHT George Sand was one of the many Parisian celebrities to whom Dickens was introduced. A fellow writer, she lived her life in a truly Bohemian and feminist fashion.

During his time in Paris, Dickens was writing *Little Dorrit* and making copious research notes that would prove vital for *A Tale of Two Cities*. He was also fretting about the state of his marriage. Enforced proximity in the small apartment made him increasingly irritable with Catherine: in London, she had her own circle of acquaintance and social life; in Paris, she was more reliant on him and he found her presence cloying.

Other problems he had hoped to free himself from had simply followed him from London, not least the discovery that the begging-letter writers who so plagued him in London had equally as many counterparts in Paris. In a letter to Wilkie Collins written from Paris, Dickens complained about the number of people who begged him for money:

Every Frenchman who can write a begging letter writes one, and leaves it for this apartment. He first of all buys any literary composition printed in quarto on tea-paper with a limp cover, scrawls upon it "Hommage à Charles Dickens, l'illustre Romancier" – encloses the whole in a dirty envelope, reeking with tobacco smoke – and prowls, assassin-like, for days, in a big cloak ... about the scraper of the outer door.

The Dickens family stayed in Paris until the end of May 1856. They then spent the summer in Boulogne.

29

LITTLE DORRIT

Dickens's next novel touched deeply on his own experiences, although few people would realize it during his lifetime. "Little Dorrit" is the nickname of Amy Dorrit, "the child of the Marshalsea", who was born in the debtors' prison.

By the time Dickens started writing *Little Dorrit*, the Marshalsea had been closed for over a decade, so he set the tale in the 1820s, the same decade in which his own family had been imprisoned there.

The novel was published in monthly parts, with the first episode appearing in time for Christmas 1855. Although the critics were not favourably impressed, the public loved the new story. *Blackwood's Magazine* may have dismissed the new serial as "twaddle", but *Little Dorrit* outsold all Dickens's previous serials. It ran for a year and a half, with the author writing it while travelling between London, Kent and France, including his time living in Paris.

Numerous characters in *Little Dorrit* are instantly memorable – among them the furiously jealous Tattycoram, the murderous Rigaud, the enigmatically moody Miss Wade and the secretive and ruinous Mr Merdle. The worlds contained in the novel are varied and fascinating: the poverty that enmeshes Bleeding Heart Yard and the prison; the mystery of Mrs Clennam's house, which seems to speak and groan to the terrified servant, Affery; the fabulous backdrop to the Dorrits' sumptuous overseas travels; and one of the author's most fantastic inventions, the Circumlocution Office.

The main strand of the plot follows the course of the Dorrit family's life, from abject poverty, shame and imprisonment to release, riches and snobbery. The only one of the family to remain true to their ideals is Amy, the child born in the prison. *Little Dorrit* is also the story of Arthur Clennam – a man whose life is continually blighted by the malignant hatred shown to him by his mother – and of all those who come into contact with the Circumlocution Office, the

ABOVE One of the tall, forbidding walls that enclosed the Marshalsea Prison. The gaol was closed in 1842.

OPPOSITE An 1857 engraving by Phiz showing Arthur Clennam escorting Flora Finching around his mother's home, accompanied by Jeremiah and Affery Flintwinch.

LITTLE DORRIT

BY

CHARLES DICKENS.

LONDON:

BRADBURY & EVANS, BOUVERIE STREET.

1857.

Marshalsea Prison and the careless machinations of Mr Merdle and his circle.

Little Dorrit allowed Dickens to vent his feelings about so many injustices and pet causes. The Merdles are his attack on snobbery and the class system, the Marshalsea is his attack on a society that allows people to sink to such depths without help, and the ridiculous Flora Finching is his revenge on Maria Beadnell, the girl who broke his heart more than two decades previously.

While he was writing *Little Dorrit*, travelling extensively, writing articles and giving public readings, Dickens was also striving to help a young woman named Caroline Thompson. After her lover abandoned Caroline and their baby, she was left destitute and had no financial option other than to turn to prostitution. In desperation, her younger brother, Frederick Maynard, wrote to the author, knowing of him as a charitable man concerned with the plight of women, a philanthropist who had set up Urania Cottage with Angela Burdett-Coutts as a home for "friendless women". Dickens was so moved by Caroline's story and so impressed with her personality that he befriended her and her child and tried to help her find work. After his first meeting with Caroline he wrote in a letter, "I cannot get the picture of her out of my head." Caroline Thompson is often cited as the inspiration for the meek, sensible character of Amy Dorrit.

The novel, which Dickens initially named *Nobody's Fault*, was written during a very turbulent time in the author's life: his marriage was slowly dying and he was uncertain of what his future held. Partly for this reason, but also because of the childhood memories that the plot conjured up, *Little Dorrit* is one of Dickens's darkest, least humorous novels. Even when he was part way through the novel, the author was still unsure in which direction he should lead his latest plot.

OPPOSITE This illustration by Phiz is for the title page of the novel. Little Dorrit can be seen stepping through a doorway at the Marshalsea Prison.

Preface to Little Dorrit

When *Little Dorrit* was published as a complete book in June 1857, Dickens included a preface which contained the following words:

Some of my readers may have an interest in being informed whether or no any portions of the Marshalsea Prison are yet standing. I did not know, myself, until the sixth of this present month, when I went to look ... I came to "Marshalsea Place": the houses in which I recognized, not only as the great block of the former prison, but as preserving the rooms that arose in my minds-eye when I became Little Dorrit's biographer ... whosoever goes into Marshalsea Place ... will see its narrow yard to the right and to the left, very little altered if at all, except that the walls were lowered when the place got free; will look upon rooms in which the debtors lived; and will stand among the crowding ghosts of many miserable years.

Reading the preface with the benefit of hindsight, it seems as though he was trying to reveal to his readers the deepest secret of his childhood.

30

A TALE OF TWO CITIES

During his months in Paris, Dickens used the city to research a story that had been forming in his mind. He wanted to write an historical novel set during the French Revolution. A Tale of Two Cities would not be finished until 1859, when it was published in weekly instalments in All the Year Round, but it was being created as early as 1855.

One of Dickens's primary sources for his novel was the three-volume work *The French Revolution* (1837) by historian Thomas Carlyle. The two writers knew one another well and Thomas Carlyle's wife, Jane, paid regular visits to Catherine Dickens and the two Dickens daughters. Another important element in the plotting of *A Tale of Two Cities* was a play that Dickens worked on with Wilkie Collins, *The Frozen Deep* (1857). The play revolves around two men who are in love with the same woman, and ends with one man sacrificing himself so that the other – the man with whom the woman is in love – can survive. Dickens returned to this plot device extremely effectively in *A Tale of Two Cities,* creating one of his most memorable characters, the hard-drinking, cynical, irresponsible but ultimately heroic Sydney Carton.

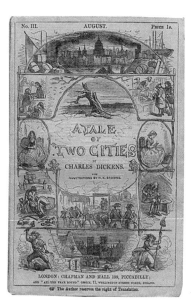

The novel begins in 1775 and spans 17 years of turmoil in Paris and peace in London. *A Tale of Two Cities* differs from many of Dickens's works by relying more on historical accuracy and lyrically beautiful writing than on the expected Dickensian humour. It is a story of love, conflict, betrayal, revenge and sacrifice, of the fickle fortunes that followed aristocrats and peasants alike during the years of the French Revolution.

Lucie Manette, the novel's heroine, is an archetypal Dickensian woman: young, beautiful and adored. There has often been speculation that Lucie, "a young lady of not more than seventeen ... a short, slight,

LEFT A cover from the August instalment of *A Tale of Two Cities.* The novel was published in monthly parts from April to November 1859.

pretty figure, a quantity of golden hair, a pair of blue eyes that met his own", was based on Dickens's mistress, the actress Ellen Ternan. Dickens met Ellen for the first time in 1857, when she auditioned to appear in *The Frozen Deep*. By the time he was writing *A Tale of Two Cities*, he had separated from his wife of 20 years and had become obsessed by the beauty and youth of his mistress. In this work, Lucie is "the golden thread" that holds the story together.

The novel contains some of the most memorable lines ever penned by Charles Dickens, including one of the most famous openings of any novel in the English language: "It was the best of times, it was the worst of times, it was the age of wisdom, it was the age of foolishness...".

ABOVE *The Battle of Valmy, 20th September 1792* by Jean-Baptiste Mauzaisse. The battle was the French army's first major victory during the French Revolution.

LEFT Thomas Carlyle (1795–1881), author of *The French Revolution*. The book was one of Dickens's primary reference sources when writing *A Tale of Two Cities*.

THE END OF THE MARRIAGE

As Charles's fame grew, so did his workload, his responsibilities and his air of celebrity. As his personality expanded, so Catherine's seemed to diminish, and they moved increasingly far apart. Catherine disliked the amount of time he spent working and he disliked what he perceived as her inherently lazy nature.

The marriage was obviously under strain and Charles's all-consuming excitement upon hearing from Maria Winter (née Beadnell) in 1855 emphasizes how desperately he was craving affection and excitement. His disappointment in discovering that Maria, like Catherine, had grown middle-aged and fat exemplifies Dickens's inability to accept the realities of life. Although his mirror must have told him he, too, had aged considerably since he had last seen Maria, he was bitterly disappointed at what felt like losing his young lover all over again.

By the time he met, and became besotted by, Ellen Ternan in 1857, Charles was longing for the excitement and passion of his youth. For Catherine, the crisis came in a deeply humiliating fashion. Charles had ordered from his usual jeweller a bracelet for Ellen; assuming it was for Catherine, the jeweller delivered it to her at home. Charles was furious and Catherine miserable – her daughter Katey found her in tears in her room, weeping because Charles had ordered her to pay a "courtesy" visit on Mrs Ternan and her daughter. It seems he believed that if Catherine

called on the actresses, the rumours that were starting would be laid to rest – he did not seem to consider how terrible the experience would be for his wife. Perhaps he truly believed Catherine must be as indifferent to him as he was to her; he was utterly mistaken.

The separation was finally agreed in 1858. Catherine was deeply unhappy about it, but legally she had no rights – the Married Women's Property Act of 1870 was over a decade away. Like many discarded wives, she found herself as much a victim of the legal system and the mores of polite society as she was of her husband.

Catherine moved into a house near Regent's Park, close to her sister Helen and her parents. She received an income of £600 a year from her estranged husband. Financially she had few complaints, but emotionally and morally she had many. Dickens tried to insist that all the children stay living with him (as was usual – and legally

OPPOSITE This photograph of Dickens was taken by Herbert Watkins in 1858, the year in which the author separated from his wife. Watkins had a fashionable photographic studio in London's Regent Street.

enforceable – at this date, despite the fact that little Plorn was only six years old). Their eldest son, Charley, now an adult and working at Barings Bank, refused and moved in with his mother. Catherine missed her children terribly. At her new home she would hold parties for local children, parties which her own young children were unable to attend. With the exception of Charley, and Katey – who defied her father to visit her mother, albeit infrequently – the Dickens children barely saw their mother again. When Walter, Frank, Alfred and Plorn were sent to live abroad, Catherine was not even consulted.

In the aftermath, Dickens became incensed by rumours that were reaching him of his cruel treatment of his wife and salacious enquiries as to why the separation had occurred. In a move that demonstrates how emotionally disturbed he was, he wrote a letter about the breakdown of the marriage to a friend in America, Arthur Smith, and published a "statement" in *Household Words*. Dickens later claimed that the letter to Smith was never intended for publication and referred to it ever after as "the violated letter" (it was published in the New York papers and soon made its way into the papers in England). Both the letter and the statement referred to the marriage breakdown and alluded to Catherine's mental instability and how "miserable" he, Catherine and their children had been for many years. In *Household Words*, he insisted his "domestic trouble" had been "long-standing" and wrote of "wicked" people spreading untrue rumours. However, Dickens was well aware of the nature of the

media, and there's every chance he knew the letter would end up being published.

Ever since the 1850s, people have queried why Georgina Hogarth sided against her sister. It must have been an impossible situation for her. She loved the children as much as their parents did: she had brought up the youngest five since their births, as Catherine was often too incapacitated to be able to care for them. If she had returned to her parents' home, Georgina would have lived a dull, relatively impecunious, spinster's life. At the age of 37, she would have been far too old to make a good marriage and have children of her own. By staying with Dickens, she remained with the children she loved, lived in a beautiful home with no financial worries, had an exciting social life – and stayed in her role as formidable housekeeper to the most famous man in the country. The question of why she was willing to betray her sister, however, continues to fuel debate.

Seven years after Dickens's death, Catherine realized she had cancer. Her daughter Katey, to whom Aunty Georgy had been "a second mother", arranged a meeting between the estranged sisters: ostensibly the two women forgave each other and cried together. It is, however, interesting that in her will Catherine bequeathed to Georgina a ring that had been a present from Count d'Orsay – a ring in the shape of a snake. Catherine died in 1879 and is buried in Highgate Cemetery in London, where she shares a grave with her baby daughter Dora, who died in 1851.

The Rift with Thackeray

The first time Charles Dickens heard the name William Makepeace Thackeray (1811–63) was after the suicide of the illustrator Robert Seymour. Not yet set on his course as a novelist, Thackeray applied (unsuccessfully) to be the new illustrator of *The Pickwick Papers*. Dickens and Thackeray soon became friends and literary rivals – although their friendship was not always easy.

The friendship between the two men had already cooled in 1857, after a young friend of Dickens, the graspingly ambitious journalist Edmund Yates, wrote a scathing article about Thackeray. Despite the justifiable anger felt by his more longstanding friend, Dickens did not support Thackeray in his mission to see Yates expelled from the Garrick Club, to which they all belonged. To add to the problem, in 1858, when Dickens was trying to keep Ellen Ternan's name out of the scandal surrounding the end of his marriage, Thackeray inadvertently made things worse. Popular gossip was whispering that Catherine's sister Georgina was Dickens's mistress. As a friend of Georgina's, Thackeray was overheard trying to protect her reputation and explaining that Dickens's mistress was an actress. Dickens was incensed. Thackeray's view of the marriage breakdown was expressed in a letter to his mother: "To think of the poor matron [Catherine] after 22 years of marriage going away out of her house! Oh dear me it's a fatal story for our trade."

Dickens refused to have anything to do with Thackeray for almost five years. His daughters were deeply upset as they adored Thackeray and his daughters. In 1863, shortly before Thackeray's very sudden and early death, Katey engineered a meeting between the estranged friends, at which the rift was healed.

RIGHT The Dickens family moved into Tavistock House in 1851. They were living here when the marriage finally broke down, and when Dickens wrote *Bleak House*, *Hard Times* and *Little Dorrit*.

OPPOSITE LEFT The many years of pregnancies and childrearing took their toll on Catherine Dickens's health and on her looks.

OPPOSITE RIGHT Maria Beadnell broke Dickens's heart when he was a teenager. When she came back into his life in 1855, he was filled with the excitement his marriage no longer held. The middle-aged Maria was, however, a disappointment.

GAD'S HILL PLACE

In 1855, WH Wills (Charles Dickens's editor and close friend) attended
a dinner party where he met a woman named Eliza Lynn, who told him
about a property she had inherited from her parents, a house in Kent that she
was eager to sell. It was a fateful coincidence: Wills had heard Dickens talk
about the same house many times.

In his collection of sketches known as *The Uncommercial Traveller*, Dickens related his childhood remembrance of this very same house. The story is autobiographical, but Dickens wrote about it in the third person, as an experience related by a "very queer small boy":

When I was not more than half as old as nine, it used to be a treat for me to be brought to look at it [the house]. And now, I am nine, I come by myself to look at it. And ever since I can recollect, my father, seeing me so fond of it, has often said to me, if you were to be very persevering and were to work hard, you might come some day to live in it.

At the time of the dinner party, the Dickens family were living in Paris; Wills wrote to Dickens immediately and was instructed to buy the house. Within months the author was the owner of the house he called Gad's Hill Place, as well as 26 acres of surrounding land, including a "wilderness" that stood on the other side of the road from the garden. After moving into the house, Dickens paid for a tunnel to be built underneath the road, so that he could walk freely around his property without risking running into eager fans or journalists as he crossed the road.

Initially, the house in Kent was intended as a second home, as the family was still living at Tavistock House in London, but from 1856 onwards, they began spending increasing amounts of time at Gad's Hill Place. There were a number of spare bedrooms and rooms in which they could entertain and, when there were too many guests to be accommodated, visitors could stay at the nearby inn, the Sir John Falstaff (run by a landlord named Trood, whose name may have provided inspiration for Edwin Drood).

After Charles and Catherine Dickens separated in 1858, Gad's Hill Place became the family's main residence. It was the only house Charles Dickens ever owned and he adored it – it was the realization of his dreams. He had done exactly as his father had bid him:

OPPOSITE Photographed on the front steps of Gad's Hill Place in 1865: [standing] Katey Collins (née Dickens), Mamie Dickens and Charles Dickens. [Seated] Henry Fothergill Chorley, Charles Allston Collins (Katey's husband) and Georgina Hogarth.

LEFT Dickens's writing chalet, now closely surrounded by buildings, was originally erected in the field or "wilderness" across the road from the main house. Dickens accessed it by a private tunnel under the road.

BELOW LEFT Gad's Hill Place, at Higham, near Rochester in Kent, was the only house Charles Dickens ever owned. He bought the house in 1856 and it was here that he died in 1870.

RIGHT After moving to Gad's Hill, Dickens revelled in his position as local squire. On 26 December 1866, he hosted an elaborate "sports day" in the field his family used as a cricket pitch in the summer. He was the judge and referee – he also provided the prize money for the winners.

CHRISTMAS SPORTS,

AT
Mr. Charles Dickens's Cricket Field,
ON BOXING DAY, 1866,
To Commence at Half-past Ten to the Moment.

Open to Members of the Gadshill, Higham, Chalk, and Shorne Cricket Clubs. Entries to be made, free of all charge, with Mr. Russell, before One o'clock on Wednesday, December 19th, when the Lists will be finally closed. Colours will be distributed on the Ground.

THE FOLLOWING RACES
WILL TAKE PLACE:

100 Yards Flat — — —	First Prize 5s.;	Second Prize 2s. 6d.
120 Yards over Ten Flights of 2ft. 6in. Hurdles	First Prize 5s.;	Second Prize 2s. 6d.
440 Yards Flat — —	First Prize 10s.;	Second Prize 2s. 6d.
Twice round the Field (about 1200 Yards) —	First Prize 10s.;	Second Prize 5s.
(If a sufficient number start, a Third Prize of 2s. 6d. will be added).		
400 Yards Flat — — —	First Prize 5s.;	Second Prize 2s. 6d.
(Open only to Boys under 16 years of age, relatives of Members of the above-mentioned Clubs).		
High Jump — —	First Prize 5s.;	Second Prize 2s. 6d.
Long Jump — —	First Prize 5s.;	Second Prize 2s. 6d.
Wheelbarrow Race, blindfold, 50 Yards	First Prize 5s.;	Second Prize 2s. 6d.
Sack Race, 50 Yards — —	First Prize 5s.;	Second Prize 2s. 6d.
Three-Legged Race, 50 Yards —	First Prize 10s.;	Second Prize 2s. 6d.
(Entries for this Race to be made to MR. RUSSELL before 10 o'clock on the Morning of Running)		

Clerk of the Course	—	Mr. Charles Dickens, Jun.
Starter	— —	Mr. Marcus Stone.
Judge and Referee	—	Mr. Charles Dickens.

he had earned enough money to be able to buy the large house on the imposing hill, and he had managed to leave the city and return to Kent, the countryside for which he had longed ever since his childhood had been disrupted by the move to London.

On 17 July 1860, Katey Dickens married the Pre-Raphaelite artist Charles Allston Collins, younger brother of Wilkie Collins, at the church in Higham. Dickens hired a special train to bring guests from London, and visitors descended on Gad's Hill Place and the Sir John Falstaff inn. The wedding caused great excitement in the village, not least because a celebratory tea party had been arranged for all the local children. On the night before the ceremony, people were terrified by a series of explosions, which turned out to be the blacksmith firing a gun salute in honour of the bride, although he had neglected to warn his neighbours. As the bridal party left the church, they walked back to Gad's Hill through pathways garlanded with flowers by the villagers. After the wedding breakfast and the departure of the bride and groom, the guests played games in Dickens's garden and were driven to see the ruins of Rochester Castle and the town of Chatham before returning to Gad's Hill for croquet, dancing and supper by candlelight.

Gad's Hill is mentioned in Shakespeare's *Henry IV*, a connection which Dickens was very proud of and often mentioned to friends. Stories of events at Gad's Hill and the local area fill his letters. On 24 October 1860, he wrote to Wilkie Collins:

Rumours were brought into the house on Saturday night, that there was "a Ghost" up at Larkin's Monument. Plorn was frightened to death, and I was apprehensive of the Ghost's spreading, and coming nearer, and causing "warning" and desertion among the servants. Frank was at home, and Andrew Gordon was with us. Time, 9 o'Clock. Village talk and credulity, amazing. I armed the two

boys with a stout stick apiece, and shouldered my double-barrelled gun, well loaded with shot. "Now observe," says I to the domestics, "if anybody is playing tricks, and has got a head, I'll blow it off." Immense impression. New groom is obviously convinced that he has entered the service of a blood thirsty demon.

Led by Dickens, the party ascended to the local monument: the ghost turned out to be "an asthmatic sheep".

Desperate to escape the bustle of family life and to write in peace – as well to avoid the large numbers of often unexpected visitors – Dickens built a special place in which to write. It was a Swiss chalet, built in the "wilderness" and accessible through the tunnel. The chalet was a gift from his friend, the actor Charles Fechter (1824–79), and caused great hilarity when it arrived by boat in 94 pieces, accompanied by one of Fechter's French servants, whose job was to construct the little building. It was at his desk in this chalet, working on *The Mystery of Edwin Drood*, that Charles Dickens would spend the last day of his life.

ABOVE Charles Dickens in his study at Gad's Hill Place. The bookcase behind him is fake; it is actually a door which Dickens had made especially for Tavistock House in London and which he brought with him to Kent.

THE GREAT INTERNATIONAL WALKING-MATCH

Of February 29, 1868.

The origin of this highly exciting and important event cannot be better stated than in the articles of agreement subscribed by the parties.

THE ARTICLES

Articles of Agreement entered into at Baltimore, in the United States of America, this Third day of February in the year of our Lord one thousand eight hundred and sixty-eight, between GEORGE DOLBY, British Subject, *alias* the Man of Ross, and JAMES RIPLEY OSGOOD, American Citizen, *alias* the Boston Bantam.

Whereas, some Bounce having arisen between the above men in reference to feats of pedestrianism and agility, they have agreed to settle their differences and prove who is the better man, by means of a walking-match for two hats a side and the glory of their respective countries; and whereas they agree that the said match shall come off, whatsoever the weather, on the Mill Dam road outside Boston on Saturday, the Twenty-ninth day of this present month; and whereas they agree that the personal attendants on themselves during the whole walk, and also the umpires and starters and declarers of victory in the match shall be JAMES T. FIELDS of Boston, known in sporting circles as Massachusetts Jemmy, and CHARLES DICKENS of Falstaff's Gad's Hill, whose surprising performances (without the least variation) on that truly national instrument, the American Catarrh, have won for him the well-merited title of The Gad's Hill Gasper.

Now, these are to be the articles of the match:—

1. The men are to be started, on the day appointed, by Massachusetts Jemmy and The Gasper.
2. Jemmy and The Gasper are, on some previous day, to walk out at the rate of not less than four miles an hour by the Gasper's watch, for one hour and a half. At the expiration of that one hour and a half, they are to carefully note the place at which they halt. On the match's coming off, they are to station themselves in the middle of the road, at that precise point, and the men (keeping clear of them and of each other) are to turn round them, right shoulder inward, and walk back to the starting-point. The man declared by them to pass the starting-point first is to be the victor and the winner of the match.
3. No jostling or fouling allowed.
4. All cautions or orders issued to the men by the umpires, starters, and declarers of victory, to be considered final and admitting of no appeal.

5. A sporting narrative of the match to be written by The Gasper within one week after its coming off, and the same to be duly printed (at the expense of the subscribers to these articles) on a broadside. The said broadside to be framed and glazed, and one copy of the same to be carefully preserved by each of the subscribers to these articles.
6. The men to show on the evening of the day of walking, at six o'clock precisely, at the Parker House, Boston, when and where a dinner will be given them by The Gasper. The Gasper to occupy the chair, faced by Massachusetts Jemmy. The latter promptly and formally to invite, as soon as may be after the date of these presents, the following Guests to honor the said dinner with their presence: that is to say:—Mistress Annie Fields, Mr. Charles Eliot Norton and Mrs. Norton, Professor James Russell Lowell and Mrs. Lowell and Miss Lowell, Doctor Oliver Wendell Holmes and Mrs. Holmes, Mr. Howard Malcom Ticknor and Mrs. Ticknor, Mr. Aldrich and Mrs. Aldrich, Mr. Schlesinger, and an obscure poet named Longfellow (if discoverable) and Miss Longfellow.

Now, Lastly, In token of their accepting the trusts and offices by these articles conferred upon them, these articles are solemnly and formally signed by Massachusetts Jemmy and by the Gad's Hill Gasper, as well as by the men themselves.

Signed by the Man of Ross, otherwise

Signed by the Boston Bantam, otherwise

Signed by Massachusetts Jemmy, otherwise

Signed by The Gad's Hill Gasper, otherwise

Witness to the signatures.

THE SPORTING NARRATIVE

THE MEN.

The Boston Bantam (*alias* Bright Chanticleer) is a young bird, though too old to be caught with chaff. He comes of a thorough game breed and has a clear though modest crow. He pulls down the scale at ten stone and a half and add a pound or two. His previous performances in the Pedestrian line have not been numerous. He once achieved a neat little match against time in two left boots at Philadelphia; but this must be considered as a pedestrian eccentricity, and cannot be accepted by the rigid chronicler as high art. The old mower with the scythe and hour-glass has not yet laid his mawley heavily on the Bantam's frontispiece, but he has had a grip at the Bantam's top feathers, and in plucking out a handful was very near making him like the great Napoleon Bonaparte (with the exception of the victualling-department), when the ancient one found himself too much occupied to carry out the idea, and gave it up. The Man of Ross (*alias* old Alick Pope, *alias* Allourpraiseswhyshouldlords, &c.) is a thought and a half too fleshy, and, if he accidentally sat down upon his baby, would do it to the tune of fourteen stone. This popular Codger is of the rubicund and jovial sort, and has long been known as a piscatorial pedestrian on the banks of the Wye. But Izaak Walton had n't Pace,—look at his book and you 'll find it slow,—and when that article comes in question, the fishing-rod may prove to some of his disciples a rod in pickle. Howbeit, the Man of Ross is a Lively Ambler and has a smart stride of his own.

THE TRAINING.

If Brandy Cocktails could have brought both men up to the post in tip-top feather, their condition would have left nothing to be desired. But both might have had more daily practice in the poetry of motion. Their breathings were confined to an occasional Baltimore burst under the guidance of the Gasper, and to an amicable toddle between themselves at Washington.

THE COURSE.

Six miles and a half, good measure, from the first tree on the Mill Dam road, lies the little village (with no refreshments in it but five oranges and a bottle of blacking) of Newton Centre. Here Massachusetts Jemmy and the Gasper had established the turning-point. The road comprehended every variety of inconvenience to test the mettle of the men, and nearly the whole of it was covered with snow.

THE START

was effected beautifully. The men, taking their stand in exact line at the starting-post, the first tree aforesaid, received from The Gasper the warning, "Are you ready?" and then the signal, "One, two, three. Go!" They got away exactly together, and at a spinning speed, waited on by Massachusetts Jemmy and The Gasper.

THE RACE.

In the teeth of an intensely cold and bitter wind before which the snow flew fast and furious across the road from right to left, The Bantam responded to the challenge and soon breasted him. For the first three miles, each led by a yard or so alternately; but the walking was very even. On four miles being called by The Gasper, the men were side by side; and then ensued one of the best periods of the race, the same splitting pace being held by both, through a heavy snow-wreath and up a dragging hill. At this point it was anybody's game, a dollar on Rossius and two half-dollars on the member of the feathery tribe. When five miles were called, the men were still shoulder to shoulder. At about six miles, the Gasper put on a tremendous spirt to leave the men behind and establish himself as the turning-point at the entrance of the village. He afterwards declared that he received a mental knock-downer, on taking his station and facing about, to find Bright Chanticleer close in upon him, and Rossius steaming up like a Locomotive. The Bantam rounded first; Rossius rounded wide; and from that moment the Bantam steadily shot ahead. Though both were breathed at the turn, the Bantam quickly got his bellows into obedient condition, and blew away like an orderly Blacksmith in full work. The forcing-pumps of Rossius likewise proved themselves tough and true, and warranted first-rate, but he fell off in pace; while the Bantam pegged away with his little drum-sticks, as if he saw his wives and a peck of barley waiting for him at the family perch. Continually gaining upon him of Ross, Chanticleer gradually drew ahead within a very few yards of half a mile, finally doing the whole distance in two hours and forty-eight minutes. Ross had ceased to compete, three miles short of the winning-post, but bravely walked it out, and came in seven minutes later.

REMARKS.

The difficulties under which this plucky match was walked can only be appreciated by those who were on the ground. To the excessive rigour of the icy blast, and the depth and state of the snow, must be added the constant scattering of the latter into the air and into the eyes of the men, while heads of hair, beards, eyelashes, and eyebrows, were frozen into icicles. To breathe at all, in such a rarefied and disturbed atmosphere, was not easy; but to breathe up to the required mark was genuine, slogging, dingdong, hard labor. That both competitors were game to the backbone, doing what they did under such conditions, was evident to all; but, to his gameness, the courageous Bantam added unexpected endurance, and (like the sailor's watch that did three hours to the cathedral clock's one) unexpected powers of going when wound up. The knowing eye could not fail to detect considerable disparity between the lads; Chanticleer being, as Mrs. Cratchit said of Tiny Tim, "very light to carry," and Rossius promising fair to attain the rotundity of the Anonymous Cove in the epigram:

"And when he walks the streets the paviors cry,
'God bless you, sir!' and lay their rammers by."

ABOVE This humorous sporting narrative of a burlesque walking match between Dolby "the Man of Ross" (Dickens's Reading Tour Manager) and Osgood "the Boston Bantam" (a junior partner in the firm of Dickens's American publishers), was written by Dickens who, with Fields "Massachusetts Jemmy", umpired the contest which took place in Boston on 29th February 1868. In it he refers to himself as the "Gad's Hill Gasper" on account of his "surprising performances (without the least variation), on that truly national instrument, the American catarrh". Osgood was the winner, walking the course over the Mill Dam Road from Boston to Newton Centre and back at a brisk pace.

OPPOSITE BOX This copy of Dickens's Christmas novella *The Chimes: A Goblin Story* is inscribed: "Hans Christian Andersen from his friend and admirer Charles Dickens. London July 1847".

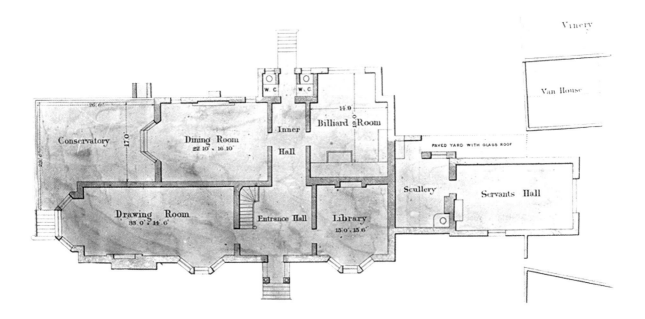

ABOVE This floor plan of Gad's Hill Place was made after Dickens's death. It shows the outbuildings as well as the house, including the vinery.

Andersen's Visit

In the summer of 1857, Danish author Hans Christian Andersen arrived at Gad's Hill. The two authors had met ten years previously and begun a warm correspondence. When Andersen was invited to visit for a fortnight, he wrote a letter promising "I shall not inconvenience you too much". That letter would come to seem highly ironic when he prolonged his stay to five weeks – a time which, in the words of Dickens, "seemed to the family AGES". Catherine Dickens took pity on the guest her husband had grown tired of and tried to think up outings to keep him entertained. The Dickens children found Andersen extremely odd and he particularly offended Charley by telling him that in Denmark it was the custom of the eldest son to shave honoured guests in the morning. Charley refused. The children were also shocked when, after receiving a letter from home with a bad review of his latest story, Andersen lay on the lawn and cried. Andersen's letters to the Queen of Denmark about his exciting stay with Charles Dickens are a sad comparison to the relief felt by the Dickens family when he finally departed.

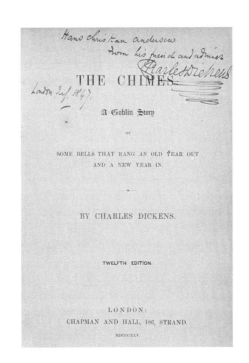

33

GREAT EXPECTATIONS

"Such a very fine, new, and grotesque idea has opened upon me," wrote Dickens on first conceiving his idea for what would become Great Expectations, *published in 1860–61. The story of Pip, Estella, Miss Havisham and Magwitch is a story of the social class system, of the judicial system, of misery and abuse – and of love, in many of its varied forms.*

The orphaned Pip lives with his abusive sister and gentle brother-in-law, Mr and Mrs Joe Gargery. Mrs Joe brings Pip up "by hand", an expression Pip thinks must relate to the constant beatings she dishes out, both to him and her husband.

Estella, also believed to be an orphan, is being brought up by the wealthy recluse Miss Havisham. Unlike Pip, Estella has every material possession, but she does not know the kind of love that Pip receives from Joe and their friend Biddy. *Great Expectations* is one of Dickens's most psychologically complex novels and Miss Havisham is one of his most magnificent creations, a truly memorable and tragic figure. Once a carefree young heiress, she was jilted when her fiancé not only left her but deceived her and stole her money, aided and abetted by her brother. She has remained frozen in time, since the moment she received her fiancé's letter. The clocks have

all been stopped, the wedding breakfast still lies on the table, slowly being devoured by mice and insects, and Miss Havisham remains in her now-tattered wedding clothes. Her home, the residence of a woman whose thirst for vengeance can never be satisfied, is the aptly named Satis House – within its walls, Estella is being brought up to despise all men and to break their hearts.

There are several possible sources from which Dickens could have drawn inspiration for Miss Havisham. One was the Australian case, which had appeared in British newspapers, of Miss Eliza Emily Donnithorne, who was jilted at the altar and became a famous recluse. The other was a popular London story

ABOVE Many composers were inspired to create songs to accompany Dickens's novels. This ballad was inspired by the plot of *Great Expectations*.

about the eighteenth-century merchant Nathaniel Bentley, nicknamed "Dirty Dick". When his fiancée died the night before their wedding, Nathaniel had a mental breakdown. He closed off most of the rooms in his home, including that in which the wedding breakfast was laid out, and refused ever to wash again. Another inspiration for the character of Miss Havisham was the legendary "White Woman" always dressed as a bride, who was a well-known sight around Berners Street in London's Soho. Dickens also wrote about her in *Household Words* in 1853, in an article entitled "Where We Stopped Growing".

Great Expectations begins with Pip in the graveyard, sobbing over the graves of his parents and five brothers. Suddenly he encounters a terrifying apparition, a yelling fury of a man with a convict's iron attached to his leg, who threatens to cut Pip's throat and eat him piece by piece. The man orders him to bring a file, food and drink: Magwitch has burst into the novel, an almost inhuman figure at this first meeting, yet one who will orchestrate much of the action from behind the scenes.

The theme of abuse runs all the way through the novel. Magwitch has been abused by life and the legal system. Mrs Joe beats Joe and Pip and is, in turn, attacked by an unknown assailant, after which she is forced to remain trapped inside a useless body. Miss Havisham was bullied and abused by the men in her life, so she trains Estella to treat others with cruelty and contempt. As Estella breaks Pip's heart, she paves the way for her own unpleasant fate. Estella's life is wrecked by love and its consequences: from her unknown murderer mother and unknown criminal father to the insane woman who adopts her and the violent husband who beats and abuses her. It is unsurprising that Dickens's initial idea was to leave the novel without his customary happy ending.

Happy Ever After

Initially, the ending of *Great Expectations* was very different from the one known today. Dickens veered away from his usual practice by not permitting Pip and Estella a happy ending; instead they meet unexpectedly, glimpse their mutual unhappiness, yet are powerless to change one another's lives. It was Dickens's friend Edward Bulwer Lytton (1803–73), a fellow novelist, who persuaded the author to change it. In a letter to John Forster, Dickens wrote, "I have put in as pretty a little piece of writing as I could, and I have no doubt that the story will be more acceptable through the alteration." This new ending sees Pip visiting Miss Havisham's destroyed home. By chance, Estella is already there, as if waiting for him. They talk, then Pip takes Estella's hand and leads her away from the ruin of Satis House. The final words belong to Pip: "I saw no shadow of another parting from her."

ABOVE LEFT Restoration House in Rochester, Kent, dates back to the seventeenth century. When Dickens wrote about Miss Havisham's home, Satis House, he was basing it on Restoration House.

ABOVE In the nineteenth century, prison ships were a common sight off the English coast. Like Magwitch in *Great Expectations*, the criminals inside were awaiting transportation to Australia.

34

ELLEN TERNAN

Ellen Lawless Ternan (1839–1914), known as "Nelly", was born into a family of actors. Her father died while Ellen was still a child, so she, her two older sisters and their mother needed to earn enough money to support themselves. Mrs Ternan was a consummate actress, and Ellen and her sisters Maria and Fanny were fairly popular, although none were destined for fame.

Fanny's ultimate dream was to be a singer; the family's association with Charles Dickens would permit this dream to become a reality.

In 1857, Charles Dickens and Wilkie Collins were enjoying theatrical acclaim with Collins's play *The Frozen Deep*. It was so successful – Queen Victoria demanded a special royal performance – that Dickens decided to take it on tour. To perform in public theatres, in "the provinces", he knew he would need to hire professional actresses for the roles currently being performed by his daughters and sisters-in-law. When Mrs Ternan and her daughters were recommended to him he auditioned them, and almost immediately became infatuated with 18-year-old Ellen. Charles Dickens was 45. Ellen was the same age as his younger daughter, Katey.

Dickens's affair with Ellen lasted for 13 years, until his death in 1870. The celebrity author managed to keep it a secret from the public, and long after his death – despite Ellen being the first beneficiary in his will – generations of Dickens scholars continue to insist the affair was nothing more than Dickens taking a "paternal" interest in the young, impecunious actress. Charles Dickens was idolized by his public, who refused to hear anything detrimental about his behaviour. Even today, his reputation continues to be revered as if he were something more than a fallible human being who fell in and out of love like everyone else; as a testament to the cult that has grown up around Charles Dickens, there are still many people who refuse to believe that Dickens ever made love to any woman except his wife.

During their affair, Dickens paid for Ellen to live in a succession of houses in what were then pretty villages outside London, including Slough and Peckham. He undertook a fascinating amount of subterfuge, paying her rent under the guise of a number of pseudonyms and seemingly enjoying the chance to be anonymous and to live this secretive, double life. When he visited the USA in 1867–68, he was desperate for Ellen to be with him, but he was persuaded by his agent and friends that it would ruin his reputation and, reluctantly, agreed she should stay at home. They did, however, spend time

ABOVE This photograph shows Ellen Ternan c.1860, shortly after she had begun her affair with Charles Dickens.

Robinson, with whom she had two children, Geoffrey and Gladys. Ellen lived out her days without ever mentioning to her family her true age or her association with Dickens. She died at the age of 75 (believed to be just 65); her story would have died with her had her son not discovered a hoard of papers which revealed not only his mother's true birthdate but that she had been an actress and the mistress of Charles Dickens. He was devastated and refused ever to hear the name of Dickens mentioned in his home again.

A few years before she died, Ellen had allegedly confessed her relationship with Dickens to a priest. Astonishingly, after her death he revealed the story she had told him in confidence. In 1928, CE Bechhofer Roberts published a novel based on the affair, entitled *This Side Idolatry*. The Dickens community was scandalized: until this time, no reference to Ellen had ever been made. Every biography of the author had carefully avoided mentioning her name and scholars studiously avoided interviewing the Ternans or anyone who had known them, in an effort to keep his reputation spotless.

In 1939, almost 70 years after Dickens's death, Gladys Storey (née Robinson) published *Dickens and Daughter*, her account of ten years of weekly conversations with Katey. She revealed that Katey (who had died in 1929) had told her of the affair and that Ellen had given birth to Dickens's baby, a son who died very soon after his birth. Although Katey and her brother Henry both mentioned the existence of this baby boy, some Dickens scholars even today persist in claiming they were lying – although why Charles Dickens's children would have chosen to lie about something as important as this has never been explained.

After reading *Dickens and Daughter*, Sir Henry Fielding Dickens's widow, Marie, wrote to Gladys Storey:

As for the silly Beadnall love affair and the Ternan affair every one has heard these stories over and over again, 4 generations know about it, published in letters, in books and in papers, and now you give it to a 5th generation! Every one of these people are no more. Why not speak only of Charles Dickens for the good he did to the poor & to the sufferers. His books belong to all, but his private life to himself alone, and I wish, oh how I wish that these blemishes & shortcomings of this great writer, should be unmentioned once and for all.

together over the years in Condette, a village outside Boulogne, where it is believed that Ellen gave birth to a baby boy, who sadly died.

After Dickens's death, Ellen was left in turmoil. She had never been a remarkable actress onstage, although she was to prove an exceedingly good actress offstage. In agreement with her mother and sisters, she took at least a decade off her age, representing herself as barely out of her teens, meaning she need never explain what she had been doing during the years she had spent with Charles Dickens. She met, was courted by and married a respectable schoolteacher and church minister, Geoffrey

35

OUR MUTUAL FRIEND

The superbly convoluted plot and inimitable character sketches that make up
Our Mutual Friend *took Dickens almost two years to complete. The novel,*
published in monthly parts in 1864–65, begins with an eerily atmospheric
scene as Gaffer Hexam and his daughter Lizzie float along the Thames,
between Southwark and London bridges.

Gaffer is searching greedily for something, but Lizzie's face holds an expression of "horror". Before long the reader discovers that Gaffer's business is to recover victims of drowning and make money from the corpses – and what he can find in their pockets.

Our Mutual Friend deals with the themes of dirt, death and money – often in combination. The Veneerings' new-found wealth helps them to live an upwardly mobile life with little regard for anyone else; Noddy Boffin, the "golden dustman", earned his fortune from other people's rubbish; and Rogue Riderhood and Gaffer Hexam make their money from corpses. John Harmon reinvents himself after his supposed murder, trying to escape the stifling clauses of his wealthy father's will, while Bella Wilfer mourns the loss of the rich husband for whom she had longed, in the erroneous belief that money alone would make her happy.

The novel teems with subplots and fascinating characters,

including the blackmailing Silas Wegg, a one-legged poet hired by Noddy Boffin to teach him to read; Bradley Headstone, whose unrequited love for Lizzie hurls him into murderous passions; his sardonic rival, Eugene Wrayburn; and Mr Venus, a taxidermist who is passionate about human bones and constantly eyes Silas's remaining leg with a collector's greed.

Alongside this strange, often grotesque cast, Dickens created some of his most gentle characters. The tiny, disabled "Jenny Wren", a doll's dressmaker whose life has been blighted by her alcoholic father, becomes Lizzie's most loyal friend. As he had done with Oliver Twist and Little Nell, Dickens created Jenny Wren to make his readers think about the conditions in which so many children were condemned to live. Mr Riah, "a venerable man", was Dickens's

LEFT An engraving of Charles Dickens from 1869, the year before he died. He was only 57, but he looked much older. His children felt he was working himself into an early grave.

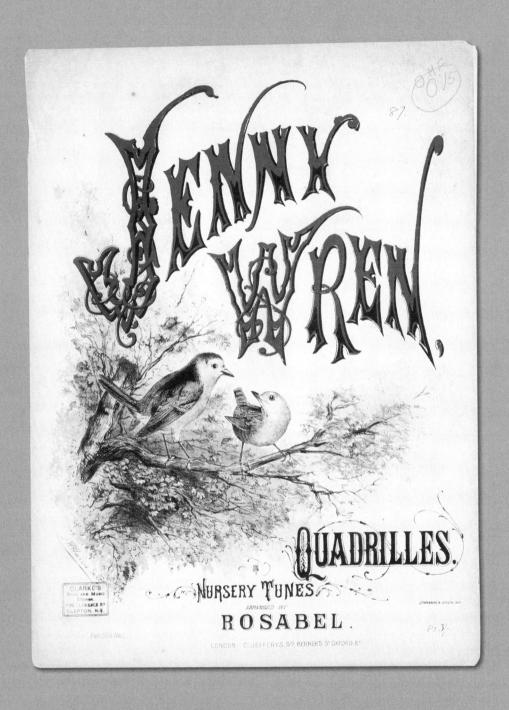

ABOVE The composers of songs and dance tunes such as this knew that if they associated their works with Dickens's writing their compositions would sell.

apology to the Jewish community for his portrayal of Fagin. Mr and Mrs Boffin are cheerful, charitable people eager to make the world a kinder place and Mr Wilfer, as well as providing the novel with humour, is often the same type of indulgent father to his adored daughter, Bella, as Dickens was to his daughters.

While he was writing *Our Mutual Friend*, Dickens experienced several personal tragedies and shocks. Shortly after beginning the novel, he discovered that his son Walter had died in India. Walter's death had occurred on 31 December 1863, but the difficulty of receiving letters from so far away meant that Dickens did not learn the news until 7 February 1864, his 52nd birthday. A few months later he was shocked to hear of the unexpected death of his good friend John Leech. Dickens's own health also began to fail around this time. By 1865, he had begun suffering such severe pain in his left foot that he was sometimes left unable to walk. A different kind of vulnerability was brought home to him about four months before he finished writing *Our Mutual Friend*, when he was involved in the

Staplehurst rail crash.

Our Mutual Friend was the last novel that Dickens would complete. Although he wrote a large number of stories and articles in between, the next novel that he would begin was the ill-fated *The Mystery of Edwin Drood*.

ABOVE An illustration by Marcus Stone of the devoted taxidermist Mr Venus, from *Our Mutual Friend* "surrounded by the trophies of his art".

Found Drowned

Nineteenth-century Londoners were used to seeing handbills requesting information about corpses pulled from the Thames, a situation portrayed with poignancy in GF Watts's painting *Found Drowned* (c.1848–50). Charles Dickens had long been haunted by these handbills and by stories he was told by the River Police in the 1850s. He recalled a policeman telling him that Waterloo Bridge was a favoured spot for suicides:

If people jump off straight forwards from the middle of the parapet of the bays of the bridge, they are seldom killed by drowning, but are smashed, poor things … you jump off from the side of the bay, and you'll tumble, true, into the stream under the arch. What you have got to do, is to mind how you jump in! There was poor Tom Steele from Dublin. Didn't dive! Bless you, didn't dive at all! Fell down so flat into the water, that he broke his breast-bone, and lived two days!

ABOVE GF Watts used painting as Dickens used writing – to expose social ills. *Found Drowned* evokes the same world Dickens conjures up in the opening scene of *Our Mutual Friend*.

36

THE STAPLEHURST CRASH

On Friday, 9 June 1865, a group of railway workers in Kent misread a train timetable. Not realizing that the boat train, which carried passengers newly arrived from France and relied on a tidal timetable, had not yet gone past, the workers left before their work on a vital railway bridge had been completed.

Charles Dickens was among the passengers on the express train from Folkestone to London. At around 3 p.m., as the train neared Staplehurst, it was going much too fast to slow down. Encountering the loosened railway plates on the bridge over the River Beult, it broke into two. Eight first-class carriages at the front of the train lurched off the bridge and into the water below. There were over 100 passengers on board, of whom ten were killed and 14 seriously injured.

Dickens was in the first of the carriages that remained on the bridge, albeit lodged in a very precarious position. Managing to force his way out of the battered carriage, Dickens, along with other survivors, tried to rescue his fellow passengers, working hard to pull the dead and dying from the wreckage. A popular magazine illustration of the day would record one of the iconic images that other passengers recalled, that of the distinguished novelist filling his hat with water and carrying it to the wounded to drink and to wash their wounds. He was also carrying a bottle of brandy in his pocket and called out to the other rescuers "I have brandy here" (brandy being supposed, at the time, to be a cure for shock). This was later reported in a newspaper as the novelist having called for someone to bring him a brandy, which amused him. Dickens persuaded the train's guards – who were rushing in a panic to try and rescue the people in the water – to give him their keys to the carriages still on the bridge so he could let trapped passengers out. Relief arrived in the form of 20 doctors who were rushed to the scene on a special train from London.

The following day Dickens wrote letters about the experience to several of his friends. As he explained to Frank Beard, "I was in the terrible accident yesterday and worked some hours among the dying and

ABOVE A depiction of the scene at Staplehurst on 9 June 1865. When the ill-fated boat train from Folkestone was derailed, there were not only ten fatalities but also 49 people injured.

OPPOSITE Charles Dickens photographed in 1865, the year of the Staplehurst rail crash. His health was affected severely by the accident and he never truly recovered from the shock.

the dead. I was in the carriage that did not go down, but hung in the air over the side of the broken bridge. I was not touched – scarcely shaken," although he goes on to explain that he feels in need of a strong sedative and is unable to sign his letter with his usual "flourish". To his friend Frederic Ouvry, Dickens commented as an aside that the accident had been "under-stated in the papers this morning". To Angela Burdett-Coutts, he wrote, in an unsteady hand, "I was in the carriage that did not go over the bridge but caught in turning and

hung suspended over the ruined brick work ... I could not have imagined so appalling a scene."

That Charles Dickens had a mistress was almost revealed in the aftermath of the crash. Ellen Ternan and her mother were travelling with him. In the panic and difficulty of escaping from the train, Ellen lost some of her jewellery. Dickens wrote to the station master at Charing Cross station, in London, asking about it: "A lady who was in the carriage with me in the terrible accident on Friday, lost ... a gold watch-chain ... a bundle of charms, a gold watch-key, and a gold seal engraved 'Ellen'." He suggested that if the items had been found they could be sent to him and he would return them to the lady. His letter suggested she was a stranger to him, someone whose acquaintance he had made because of their shared experience. What was hushed up, but must have been discussed by railway staff, was that one of the pieces was engraved to Ellen from "CD".

CHARLES DICKENS RELIEVING THE SUFFERERS AT THE FATAL RAILWAY ACCIDENT, NEAR STAPLEHURST.—SEE "GOSSIPER," PAGE 54.

The scene of the accident and his brush with mortality would scar Dickens psychologically for the rest of his life. It is notable that he even wrote a kindly letter to his estranged wife, in response to a worried letter from her, two days after the accident. In many letters written at this time he apologizes for the shakiness of his handwriting, while in others he apologizes for having dictated the letter to someone else; he also explains that he can undertake no engagements as his doctor has ordered him to rest. Some days later, he wrote a note to John Forster stating, "I am curiously weak – weak as if I were recovering from a long illness. I begin to feel it more in my head."

Having initially embraced the new technology of train travel, Dickens now found himself living in fear. He found train travel "inexpressibly distressing" and, when

ABOVE This popular illustration shows Dickens assisting the wounded after the Staplehurst rail disaster. He is pictured bringing water in his hat to an injured passenger.

possible, would use alternative transport; for a time he resorted to the old-fashioned method of travelling by boat between London and Kent, a trip which took many hours longer than the train service. During his 1867–68 journey through the USA, he suffered from increasingly poor health, exacerbated by his need to take elongated train journeys. It is not a coincidence that Dickens died, aged only 58 but utterly worn out, on the fifth anniversary of the Staplehurst crash. The accident had haunted and exhausted him for five years.

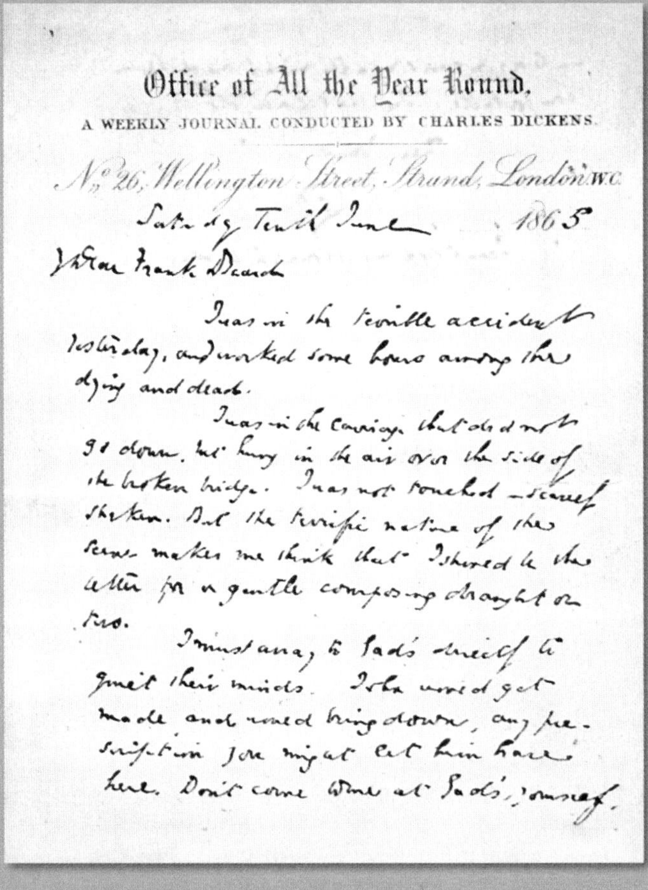

Saturday Tenth June 1865

My Dear Frank Beard

I was in the terrible accident yesterday, and worked some hours among the dying and dead.

I was in the carriage that did not go down, but hung in the air over the side of the broken bridge. I was not touched — scarcely shaken. But the terrific nature of the scene makes me think that I should be the better for a gentle composing draught or two.

I must away to Gad's directly to quiet their minds. If he would get made and send by (bring down), any prescription you might set him here. Don't come down at Gad's yourself

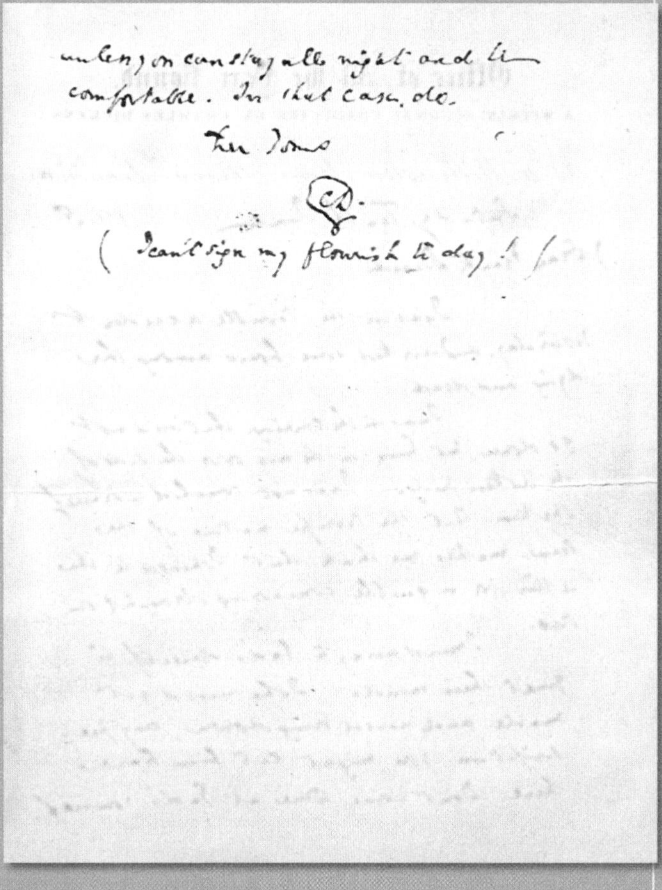

unless you can stay all night and be comfortable. In that case, do.

Ever Yours

CD.

(I can't sign my flourish to day!)

ABOVE Dickens's letter to Frank Beard, 10 June 1865 – the day after the Staplehurst crash.

37

THE READING TOURS

For many years, Dickens had read aloud from his novels to friends and in aid of charities, taking the opportunity to indulge his love of acting and to bring his characters to life. In 1858, he began a series of commercial readings. The first performance took place on Thursday 29 April at St Martin's Hall in London's Covent Garden, which was filled to capacity with an audience of 3,000 people.

The ensuing tour, arranged by Dickens's new manager, Arthur Smith, took him around England, Scotland and Ireland. Smith was adept at managing to fit as many people into venues as possible: "Arthur", wrote Dickens, "is something between a Home Secretary and a furniture dealer ... He is either always corresponding in the genteelest manner, or dragging rout seats about without his coat."

The audiences and critics were spellbound. As the *Newcastle Daily Chronicle* reported in 1858, "Mr Dickens unites uncommon dramatic power and expression, and his reading has all the interest of a well-acted play." Nine years later, Dickens remained as enthusiastic as at the start: "after hundreds of nights, I come with a feeling of perfect freshness to that little red table, and laugh and cry with my hearers, as if I had never stood there before." The reading tours led him all over the UK for almost 12 years, making him even more popular than his books had already done.

In 1861, Arthur Smith died unexpectedly; Dickens was devastated. The man whom he had described to Wilkie Collins as "all usefulness and service. I never could have done without him" seemed irreplaceable. Thomas Headland attempted to fill Smith's shoes, but the partnership was not successful. In 1866, Dickens found a new manager, George Dolby, who organized a return visit to the USA as well as managing Dickens's tours around the UK and Ireland.

During his tour of America in 1867–68, Dickens was in extremely poor health. At the start of January 1868, he wrote, "I begin at Brooklyn to-night: and thus oscillate between Philadelphia, Baltimore, and Washington, and then cut into New England, and so work my way back to Boston ... after which come Chicago, Cincinnati, Detroit and Cleveland, and Buffalo, and then Philadelphia, Boston and New York farewells." He modified his original itinerary after realizing certain journeys were going to be too gruelling – and he removed Chicago not only because of the journey but also to avoid encountering the bereaved mistress and illegitimate children of his dead brother, Augustus. The Chicago newspapers were incensed, especially as they believed Bertha and Augustus

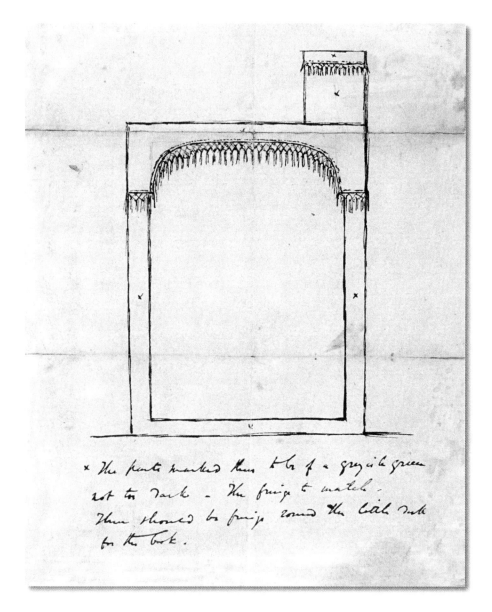

ABOVE An illustration of Charles Dickens performing a public reading, standing at the reading lectern he had designed himself. The lectern was collapsible so he could take it travelling.

LEFT Dickens drew the original design for his collapsible desk. He wanted a lectern of exactly the right height and shape to take with him on his reading tours.

had been married. For decades, the papers refused to forgive this perceived snub to their city. Well into the twentieth century, their journalists continued to write furious and usually mendacious stories about Dickens, his "sister-in-law" and her children.

The American tour exhausted the author: "I am so dead beat when I come off that they lay me down on a sofa after I have been washed and dressed, and I lie there, extremely faint, for a quarter of an hour." His letters

from America seem like those of a frail, elderly man, yet Dickens was only 55 when he embarked on the tour. His daughter Mamie was alarmed to receive a letter in April 1868 in which he described his extraordinary diet:

I cannot eat (to anything like the ordinary extent), and have established this system: At seven in the morning, in bed, a tumbler of new cream and two tablespoonsful of rum. At twelve, a sherry cobbler and a biscuit. At three (dinner time), a pint of champagne. At five minutes to

Rotunda, Dublin.

Messrs. CHAPPELL & CO. beg to announce that they have made arrangements with

MR. CHARLES DICKENS

FOR THREE

FAREWELL READINGS,

THE LAST THAT WILL EVER TAKE PLACE IN DUBLIN,

AS FOLLOWS:

On MONDAY, JANUARY 11, 1869,

On TUESDAY, JANUARY 12,

AND

On WEDNESDAY, JANUARY 13,

THE LAST READING IN DUBLIN.

On MONDAY EVENING, JAN. 11th, 1869,

MR. DICKENS WILL READ HIS

CHRISTMAS CAROL,

AND

THE TRIAL FROM PICKWICK.

On TUESDAY EVENING, JAN. 12th,

(The last Reading but one),

DAVID COPPERFIELD,

AND

MR. BOB SAWYER'S PARTY

(FROM PICKWICK).

On WEDNESDAY EVENING, JAN. 13th,

(The last Reading in Dublin),

BOOTS AT THE HOLLY TREE INN,

SIKES AND NANCY

(FROM OLIVER TWIST).

AND

MRS. GAMP.

It is scarcely necessary for Messrs. CHAPPELL and Co. to add that any announcement made in connexion with these FAREWELL READINGS will be strictly adhered to and considered final; and that on no consideration whatever will Mr. DICKENS be induced to appoint an extra night in any place in which he shall have been once announced to read for the last time.

The Readings will commence at Eight o'Clock, and be comprised within two hours.

PRICES OF ADMISSION.

Stalls (numbered and reserved), 7/

Reserved Seats, 5/   Balcony, 3/.

Admission, 1/

Tickets may be obtained of Messrs. PIGOTT and CO. at their Music Warehouse, 112, Grafton Street, where the Plan may be seen and Places secured.

ABOVE A ticket to one of Charles Dickens's readings was a very valuable item. People would queue for hours to try and buy them. Despite being made of simple card or paper, many of the tickets still survive, demonstrating how important their owners believed them.

RIGHT When preparing for his public readings, Dickens marked his books to make the text suitable for reading out loud. He would do so by highlighting or blocking out chunks of text. This extract covers the murder of Nancy by Bill Sykes in *Oliver Twist*.

OPPOSITE A crowd gathering to buy tickets to hear Charles Dickens reading at Steinway Hall in New York, during his American reading tour of 1867–68.

---

38   SIKES AND NANCY:

them, on my knees, to show the same mercy to you; and let us both leave this dreadful place, and far apart lead better lives, and forget how we have lived, except in prayers, and never see each other more. It is never too late to repent. They told me so—I feel it now. But we must have time—we must have a little, little time!"

The housebreaker freed one arm, and grasped his pistol. The certainty of immediate detection if he fired, flashed across his mind; and he beat it twice upon the up-turned face that almost touched his own.

She staggered and fell, but raising herself on her knees, she drew from her bosom a white handkerchief—Rose Maylie's—and holding it up towards Heaven, breathed one prayer for mercy to her Maker.

A READING.   39

It was a ghastly figure to look upon. The murderer staggering backward to the wall, and shutting out the sight with his hand, seized a heavy club, and struck her down. ! *Action*

The bright sun burst upon the crowded city in clear and radiant glory. Through costly-coloured glass and paper-mended window, through cathedral dome and rotten crevice, it *Mystery* shed its equal ray. It lighted up the room where the murdered woman lay. It did. He tried to shut it out, but it would stream in. If the sight had been a ghastly one in the dull morning, what was it, now, in all that brilliant light!!! / *Terror to the End* /

He had not moved; he had been afraid to stir. There had been a moan and motion of the hand; and, with terror added to rage, he had struck and struck again. Once he

eight, an egg beaten up with a glass of sherry. Between the parts the strongest beef tea that can be made, drunk hot. At a quarter-past ten, soup, and anything to drink that I can fancy. I don't eat much more than half a pound of solid food in the whole four-and-twenty hours, if so much.

Unsurprisingly, following Dickens's return to England, his family persuaded him to give up the readings – but not before, in 1869, he had embarked on a gruelling "farewell tour" through Ireland, England and Scotland. In every destination, audiences were enthralled by his account of the murder scene in *Oliver Twist*; Dickens wrote proudly to Mamie of "a contagion of fainting" among them. His children, however, were convinced that every time he recreated the brutal slaying of Nancy, he was endangering his health. By the time he started writing *Edwin Drood*, Dickens knew his body could no longer cope with the exertion of performing his readings. He gave his last performance at St James's Hall in London on 15 March 1870.

Props and Crew

Dickens designed a special reading lectern. It was essentially a collapsible travelling desk, made to exactly the right height so that it came up to his waist, allowing him to see his papers and books without being obscured from the audience. The desk, which was made of wood and covered with crimson velvet, had a small shelf attached to the side, to hold a carafe and glass. There was also a block covered in the same velvet on which to rest his book and on which he could lean if his strength was starting to fail. In addition to his manager, Dickens travelled with a lighting engineer, who understood exactly how the author wanted the stage to be lit, and a general assistant.

38

THE MYSTERY OF EDWIN DROOD

In October 1869, Dickens began writing The Mystery of Edwin Drood. *The novel is pervaded by an oppressive sense of the hopelessness, and helplessness, of opium addiction.*

Behind the usual Dickensian humour, carefully created characters and glimpses of love and humanity is a constant backdrop of menace. *The Mystery of Edwin Drood* was begun during a dark time in the novelist's life. His health was failing, he suffered regular bouts of melancholia and he was often in pain. The novel was destined to become the greatest mystery story ever written: Dickens died while writing it, leaving no notes about the ending. Although generations of scholars and dramatists have made educated suggestions, no one knows the true solution to Dickens's final mystery.

Dickens's initial thoughts, as shared with John Forster, were that he would write the story of a couple who knew each other from childhood and were betrothed very young. They would be parted and the novel would follow their destinies, with the reader and protagonists all the time aware of their "impending fate" – marriage. Soon, however, he had come up with another "very curious" idea about an

uncle who murders his nephew and writes the novel from his cell while awaiting execution. As Dickens did not plot out his story but wrote from a few notes, changing his intended plot lines as the characters progressed, it is unknown what his final thoughts were.

The first instalment was published in April 1870; it began with the drug-crazed dream of an unnamed man who gradually comes back to consciousness in the dishevelled surroundings of an opium den. The reader soon discovers that the man is John Jasper, choirmaster of Cloisterham cathedral. The city of Cloisterham was based on Rochester in Kent, not far from Dickens's home at Gad's Hill.

Edwin Drood is Jasper's nephew. He is an orphan, making his uncle, who is only a few

ABOVE Charles Dickens caricatured by Spy (the pseudonym of cartoonist Leslie Ward) in 1870. Spy drew this image just four months before the author died.

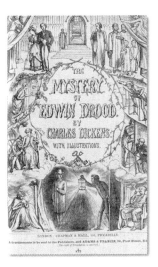

FAR LEFT A depiction of an opium den in the East End of London, c.1870. At the beginning of *The Mystery of Edwin Drood* John Jasper leaves an opium den in London.

LEFT The drawings on the front cover of *The Mystery of Edwin Drood* have been pored over by scholars even since Dickens died, hoping for a clue to the author's intentions.

years older than he, his closest relation and his guardian; the two men appear to be very close. Edwin, a student, has been engaged since childhood to Rosa Bud, the daughter of his father's best friend. Rosa, who is still at school, is also an orphan. Her relationship with Edwin is easygoing: they are more like siblings than intended lovers. John Jasper, however, is in love with Rosa; his passion is secret, guarded and intense. When the twins Neville and Helena Landless befriend Rosa and Edwin, Jasper becomes infuriated by Neville's obvious attraction to Rosa. Edwin and Rosa agree to end their engagement, but Edwin chooses not to tell his uncle – he is convinced Jasper wants him to honour his father's wishes.

When Christmas Eve arrives in Cloisterham, it is a very different kind of Christmas to those usually associated with Dickens:

Not such a power of wind has blown for many a winter night. Chimneys topple in the streets, and people hold to posts and corners, and to one another, to keep themselves upon their feet. The violent rushes abate not, but increase in frequency and fury until at midnight, when the streets are empty, the storm goes thundering along them, rattling the latches, and tearing at all the shutters, as if warning the people...

In the midst of this violent gale, Edwin Drood goes missing. A desperate search begins – but neither Edwin nor his body is to be found. Jasper claims Neville has harmed his nephew, although Neville insists on his innocence. Months go by with no word or sign of Edwin. A seemingly devastated Jasper begins to haunt both Neville and Rosa, to whom he declares his love, terrifying her in the process. Rosa turns to her guardian, Mr Grewgious, and Helena for help. Through them, she meets a new acquaintance, Mr Tartar, with whom she appears to fall in love. However, the thought of John Jasper and her fears about what could have happened to Edwin continue to plague her.

On 8 June 1870, Dickens wrote his last words of fiction. Part way through Chapter 23, which was entitled "The Dawn Again" and marked the halfway point of his planned number of chapters, he began to feel unwell. He was helped from his writing chalet back to the house to rest. That evening he suffered a stroke and never regained consciousness. He died the following day, aged 58, with several of his children – and possibly Ellen Ternan – at his side.

39

THE LEGACY OF CHARLES DICKENS

When he heard of the death of Charles Dickens, the American poet Henry Wadsworth Longfellow wrote, "It is no exaggeration to say that my whole country is stricken with grief."

In London, *The Times* commented: "Statesmen, men of science, philanthropists ... might pass away, and yet not leave the void which will be caused by the death of Dickens." The overwhelming feeling experienced by Dickens's readers was that they had lost an intimate friend. Although Dickens had requested that he be buried in Rochester Cathedral, not far from his home in Kent, Queen Victoria refused to hear of such a scheme (despite the fact that the cathedral already had the grave site prepared). The monarch insisted instead that Dickens should be laid to rest in London, in the area of Westminster Abbey known as "Poets' Corner". At 9.30 a.m. on Tuesday, 14 June 1870, a hearse and three small coaches made their way to the abbey for a very small private funeral, with the service performed by the Dean. Although *The Times* named just 13 mourners, Dickens's immediate family and closest friends, the abbey's records confirm that there were 14 mourners; it is assumed that the mystery fourteenth mourner was Ellen Ternan, her presence kept a closely guarded secret.

After the funeral, Dickens's grave was left open, so that mourners could come to see his coffin and pay their respects. Over two days, thousands of people made the pilgrimage to his grave. On the following Sunday, the Dean held a special memorial service to allow members of the public to mourn the loss of the author. His gravestone is as simple as Dickens had requested in his will that it should be: "I DIRECT that my name be inscribed in plain English letters ... without the addition of 'Mr' or 'Esquire'." In a plain typeface, the stone states simply:

CHARLES DICKENS
BORN 7th FEBRUARY 1812
DIED 9th JUNE 1870

Today, Charles Dickens remains as famous as he was in his own century. His books have spawned numerous stage, TV and film adaptations, the word "Dickensian" has become a much-used adjective and his name still retains its ability to sell newspapers. In England, there are three museums devoted to his life and works: the Charles Dickens' Birthplace Museum in Portsmouth, the Dickens House Museum in Kent and the Charles Dickens Museum

ABOVE John Everett Millais arrived at Gad's Hill Place on 10 June 1870 to discover Dickens had died in the night. He sketched this portrait of the author on his deathbed and gave it to Katey.

LEFT Although Dickens requested his grave be in Rochester Cathedral, Queen Victoria insisted that he be buried here, at Poets' Corner in London's Westminster Abbey.

Forster's Biography

Towards the end of 1871, John Forster published the first part of *The Life of Charles Dickens*. For the first time, the public, along with many of Dickens's close friends, learned about the author's childhood: his fractured education, his father's imprisonment and his time as a child labourer. Forster's biography incorporated part of Dickens's autobiography, which the author had begun while in his thirties. Dickens had abandoned it, but it had been bequeathed with his other papers to Forster.

LEFT John Forster met Charles Dickens for the first time in 1836. Forster was often jealous of the novelist's other friends and liked to be seen as the definitive authority on Dickens.

CERTIFIED COPY of an Entry in a REGISTER OF DEATHS,
(6 & 7 Wm. IV., cap. 86.)

Given at the GENERAL REGISTER OFFICE,
SOMERSET HOUSE, LONDON.

REGISTRATION DISTRICT **North Aylesford**

1870   DEATHS in the ~~Sub-~~ District of **Strood** in the County of **Kent**

No.	When and Where Died.	Name and Surname.	Sex.	Age.	Rank or Profession.	Cause of Death.	Signature, Description, and Residence of Informant.	When Registered.	Signature of Registrar.
127	Ninth June 1870 Gads Hill Place Higham	Charles Dickens	Male	58 years	Author	Apoplexy Certified	Charles Dickens Junr Present at the death 18 Gloucester Road Regents Park London.	Twelfth June 1870	Charles Saunders Registrar

CERTIFIED to be a true Copy of an Entry in the Certified Copy of a Register of Deaths in the District above mentioned.
Given at the GENERAL REGISTER OFFICE, SOMERSET HOUSE, LONDON, under the Seal of the said Office, the 4th day of December 1905.

By the Act of 6 & 7 William IV., c. 86, sec. 38, it is enacted, "That the Registrar-General shall cause to be made a Seal of the said Register Office, and the Registrar-General shall cause to be " sealed or stamped therewith all Certified Copies of Entries given in the said Office ; and all Certified Copies of Entries, purporting to be Sealed or Stamped with the Seal of the said Register Office, " shall be received as evidence of the Birth, Death, or Marriage, to which the same relates, without any further or other proof of such Entry ; and no Certified Copy purporting to be given in the said " Office shall be of any force or effect which is not Sealed or Stamped as aforesaid."
By sec. 37 of the same Act, it is enacted that, "for every general search of the Indexes shall be paid the sum of twenty shillings, and for every particular search the sum of one shilling, and for " every Certified Copy the sum of two shillings and sixpence," exclusive of Inland Revenue Stamp (33 & 34 Vict., c. 97) of one penny.
The Act 24 & 25 Vict., c. 98, sec. 36, enacts that whosoever shall "unlawfully destroy, deface, or injure, or cause or permit to be destroyed, defaced, or injured, any Register of Births, Baptisms, " Marriages, Deaths, or Burials......or any Certified Copy of any such Register, or any part thereof, or shall forge or fraudulently alter in any such Register, any Entry relating to any Birth, Baptism, " Marriage, Death, or Burial......or any Certified Copy of such Register or of any part thereof......or shall forge or counterfeit the Seal of or belonging to any Register Office......or shall offer, utter, " dispose of, or put off any such Register, Entry, Certified Copy, Certificate, or Seal, knowing the same to be false, forged, or altered," shall be guilty of Felony, and be liable to Penal Servitude, or to Imprisonment with Hard Labour.

in London. Rochester in Kent holds two Dickens Festivals every year and there are numerous other Dickens festivals held all around the world.

The legacy of Charles Dickens is perhaps best expressed by an article written during the author's lifetime. In 1868, Charles Eliot Norton (1827–1908), an American academic and writer, wrote:

No one thinks first of Mr Dickens as a writer. He is at once, through his books, a friend. He belongs among the intimates of every pleasant-tempered and large-hearted person. He is not so much the guest as the intimate of our homes. He ... helps us to celebrate Christmas with heartier cheer, he shares at every New Year in our good wishes: for, indeed, it is not in his purely literary character that he has most for us, it is as a man of the largest humanity, who has simply used literature as the means by which to bring himself into relations with his fellow-men.

ABOVE Charles Dickens's death certificate, dated 9 June 1870, stated that he died of "apoplexy". The named witness to the death was Charles Dickens Junior, the author's eldest son.

OPPOSITE BOTTOM *The Empty Chair*, by Luke Fildes, immortalized Dickens's former office. The illustrator for *The Mystery of Edwin Drood*, Fildes stayed with the family at Gad's Hill Place after Dickens's death and was inspired to sketch the author's world.

The Dickens Fellowship

The Charles Dickens Museum in London is also the headquarters of the international Dickens Fellowship, which was founded in 1902. The central aim of the Dickens Fellowship is "to knit together, in a common bond of friendship, lovers of the great master of humour and pathos, Charles Dickens". Their other aims are to spread the love of humanity, to campaign against social ills, to assist in the preservation and purchase of buildings and objects associated with Dickens, and to promote knowledge and appreciation of his works. In 1905, the Fellowship published the first issue of *The Dickensian*; it remains one of the world's foremost literary journals. Today, there are 50 branches of the Dickens Fellowship around the world.

I **Charles Dickens** of Gads Hill Place Higham in the County of Kent hereby revoke all my former Wills and Codicils and declare this to be my last Will and Testament I give the sum of £1000 free of Legacy Duty to Miss Ellen Lawless Ternan late of Houghton Place Ampthill Square in the County of Middlesex I give the sum of £19.19.0 to my faithful Servant Mrs Anne Cornelius I give the sum of £19.19.0 to the Daughter and only Child of the said Mrs Anne Cornelius I give the sum of £19.19.0 to each and every domestic Servant male and female who shall be in my employment at the time of my decease and shall have been in my employment for a not less period of time than one year I give the sum of £1000 free of legacy duty to my Daughter Mary Dickens I also give to my said Daughter Mary an annuity of £300 a year during her life if she shall so long continue unmarried, such Annuity to be considered as accruing from day to day but to be payable half yearly the first of such half yearly payments to be made at the expiration of six months next after my decease If my said Daughter Mary shall marry such annuity shall cease and in that case, but in that case only my said daughter shall share with my other Children in the provision hereinafter made for them. I give to my dear Sister in Law Georgina Hogarth the sum of £8000 free of Legacy duty I also give to the said Georgina Hogarth all my personal jewellery not hereinafter mentioned and all the little familiar objects from my writing table and my room and she will know what to do with those things I also give to the said Georgina Hogarth all my private papers whatsoever and wheresoever and I leave her my grateful blessing as the best and truest friend man ever had. I give to my eldest Son Charles, my library of printed Books and my engravings and prints. I also give to my said Son Charles the silver salver presented to me at Birmingham and the Silver Cup presented to me at Edinburgh and my shirt studs shirt pins and sleeve buttons And I bequeath unto my said Son Charles and my Son Henry Fielding Dickens the sum of £8000 Upon trust to invest the same and from time to time to vary the investments thereof and to pay the annual income thereof to my Wife during her life and after her decease the said sum of £8000 and the investments thereof shall be in trust for my Children (but subject as to my daughter Mary to the proviso hereinbefore contained) who being a son or sons shall have attained or shall attain the age of 21 years or being a daughter or daughters shall have

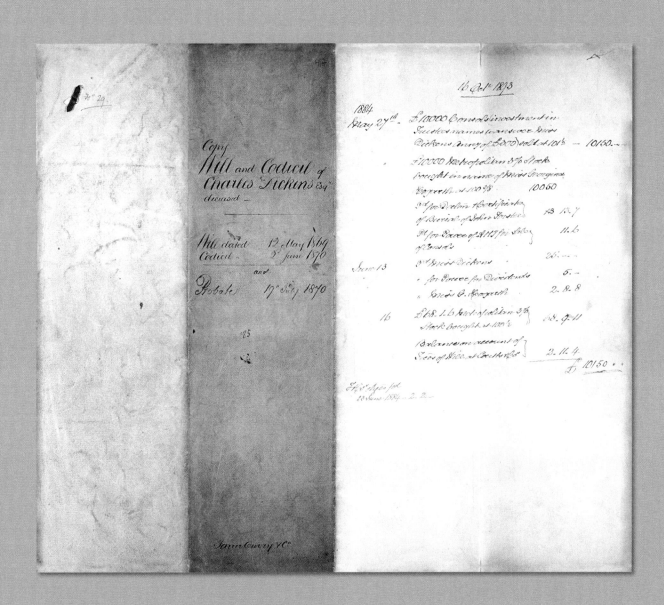

ABOVE & OPPOSITE
Dickens revised his will for the
last time exactly a week before he
died, on 2 June 1870. The first
beneficiary in the will was Ellen
Ternan, to whom he bequeathed
£1,000.

Index

(Page numbers in **bold** refer to main entries, *italic* to illustrations, photographs and captions)

Picture Credits

The publishers would also like to thank the following sources for their kind permission to reproduce the photographs in this book.

Key: t = top, b = bottom, l = left, r = right and c = centre

Charles Dickens Museum: 8tr, 9t, 9b, 12, 13c, 17, 18, 19, 21br, 22, 23t, 23bl, 25, 27, 30bl, 30r, 31, 33, 34, 35, 37, 39tl, 39tr, 40tr, 41, 42t, 42b, 43t, 43b, 44tl, 44tc, 44b, 45, 48t, 48b, 54bl, 54-55, 59tr, 61b, 62tr, 64, 65, 67, 68, 69b, 71r, 71br, 73b, 74t, 76l, 76r, 77tl, 77tr, 77br, 79, 81tr, 81br, 83, 85, 87, 89, 90l, 90r, 91, 92t, 93tl, 93tr, 93bl, 93br, 95, 96, 100l, 100r, 101, 108, 114, 117tr, 118, 122, 125, 126tl, 126tr, 127br, 130br, 132, 133t, 133br, 134, 135tl, 138, 139, 145l, 145r, 147l, 147tr, 148tl, 148tr, 148br, 151tr, 153tl, 153bl, 154b, 156, 157

Alamy: /AF Archive: 142; /Lebrecht Music and Arts Photo Library: 131, 155; /Lordprice Collection: 105, 150; /Chronicle: 7; /World History Archive: 82, 104tr

Bridgeman Images: /British Library, London, UK/ © British Library Board: 144; /Bolton Museum and Art Gallery, Lancashire, UK: 58; /Fitzwilliam Museum, University of Cambridge, UK: 97; /Guildhall Library, City of London: 21t; /Lady Lever Art Gallery, National Museums, Liverpool: 113; /Look and Learn: 26; /Museum of London, UK: 28-29; /Photo © Peter Nahum at The Leicester Galleries, London: 94; /National Gallery, London, UK: 111r; /National Trust Photographic Library: 123bc; /Private Collection: 62tl, 78, 80, 110-111, 112t, 112br, 117br, 119; /The Stapleton Collection: 109; /Victoria & Albert Museum, London, UK: 107; /Trustees of the Watts Gallery, Compton, Surrey, UK: 141br; /Wimbledon Society Museum of Local History, London, UK: 74

Carlton Books: 13br

www.clevelandstreetworkhouse.org: 49

Getty Images: /Historical Picture Archive/Corbis: 11; /Hulton Archive: 137; /Kean Collection: 129; /Rischgitz: 62br; /Oli Scarff: 130tl; /Time & Life Pictures: 115; /Universal History Archive: 123t

Mary Evans Picture Library: 8b, 15, 16, 57, 59l, 86, 92b, 103tl, 103tr, 104br, 120, 127t, 130l, 140-141, 151tl, 154tl; /Illustrated London News Ltd: 75, 143

Philip Mould and Company: 2

Science & Society Picture Library: 116

Shutterstock: /Daily Mail: 36; /Slanapotam: 4

Topfoto.co.uk: 40tl; /Fotomas: 73t; /Granger, NYC: 63, 69t, 135br, 149; /Heritage-Images: 51; /World History Archive: 61t

© V&A Images, all rights reserved: 47, 53, 71tl, 99l, 99r